RECORDS CLASSIFICATION: CONCEPTS, PRINCIPLES AND METHODS

Chandos

Information Professional Series

Series Editor: Ruth Rikowski
(email: Rikowskigr@aol.com)

Chandos' new series of books is aimed at the busy information professional. They have been specially commissioned to provide the reader with an authoritative view of current thinking. They are designed to provide easy-toread and (most importantly) practical coverage of topics that are of interest to librarians and other information professionals. If you would like a full listing of current and forthcoming titles, please visit www.chandospublishing.com.

New authors: we are always pleased to receive ideas for new titles; if you would like to write a book for Chandos, please contact Dr Glyn Jones on g.jones.2@elsevier.com or telephone +44 (0) 1865 843000.

RECORDS CLASSIFICATION: CONCEPTS, PRINCIPLES AND METHODS

Information, Systems, Context

UMI ASMA' MOKHTAR

ZAWIYAH MOHAMMAD YUSOF

Universiti Kebangsaan Malaysia

ELSEVIER

CP
CHANDOS PUBLISHING
An imprint of Elsevier

Chandos Publishing is an imprint of Elsevier
50 Hampshire Street, 5th Floor, Cambridge, MA 02139, United States
The Boulevard, Langford Lane, Kidlington, OX5 1GB, United Kingdom

British Library Cataloguing-in-Publication Data
A catalogue record for this book is available from the British Library

Library of Congress Cataloging-in-Publication Data
A catalog record for this book is available from the Library of Congress

ISBN: 978-0-08-102238-2

For information on all Chandos Publishing publications visit our website at https://www.elsevier.com/books-and-journals

Publisher: Glyn Jones
Editorial Project Manager: Peter Jardim
Production Project Manager: Mohana Natarajan
Designer: Greg Harris

Typeset by TNQ Books and Journals

CONTENTS

ABOUT THE AUTHORS

Umi Asma' Mokhtar is a senior lecturer of information science at School of Information Technology, Faculty of Information Science and Technology, Universiti Kebangsaan Malaysia. She was the recipient of the Oliver Wendell Holmes Travel Award from the Society of American Archivists in 2012. Her research interests include electronic records management, function-based classification, and information policy. She was the invited speaker at ASEAN: Records & Information Management Era in New Leadership Conference in 2010. Her papers have been published in international and national journals including the *International Journal of Information Management* and *Records Management Journal*. Currently, she is the co-researcher of InterPARES Trust project for Malaysian Team.

Zawiyah M. Yusof is a professor in Records and Information Management at the Faculty of Information Science and Technology, Universiti Kebangsaan Malaysia. She is an internationally acclaimed speaker and author of books including *Issues in Records Management* in 2005 other than published dozens of conference and journal papers. She is an internationally recognized author on the foundation of concepts and principles of records management where her articles are used by several universities offering records management courses globally. Prof. Zawiyah is a committee member for the Development of Malaysia Standard MS ISO 11799:2011 Information and Documentation – Document Storage Requirements for Archive and Library Materials [ISO 11799:2003 (2008), IDT]. As an academician in records and information management, Prof. Zawiyah leads a team of information governance research and has delivered speeches internationally and handled short courses for corporate and government institutions in her country.

PREFACE

This book introduces and discusses about classification, an element in the early stages of records life cycle. Classification ensures systematic organization of documents and facilitates information retrieval. However, classification system is not prevalent in records management compared to its use in other information field like library; in fact, both differ in terms of applications and connotations. Although classification is crucial for disposal purposes, research in the application of the concept for disposing records is still scarce as the available studies mostly concentrate on the earlier stages of the records' life cycle, i.e., the storage and retrieval.

This book views classification from the records management perspective by adopting qualitative and case study approaches involving Department of Syariah Judiciary Malaysia to gather data by means of interview and document content analysis. It was discovered that the implementation of functional records classification for electronic records is yet to be imposed, while the classification plan for conventional records is still under development; in addition, the existing records classification models are limited to discussing the activities of records' life cycle in general and conceptual manner. Such a drawback has urged the requirement for this book to develop a functional model for records classification, one that could be referred to in both the records management and the information technology (IT) fields. Current development of a records management system does not take into account the concept of classification from records management perspective. Such a model is required because the incorporation of information and communication technology (ICT) in managing records is inevitable. The concept of classification from records management perspective ought to be extended to ICT team to enable the development of a records management system which does not limit to only storage and retrieval functions but also covers the disposal and preservation process. The proposed model introduces function-based classification to ensure records are classified in context.

SCOPE OF THE TEXT

This book stresses the requirement for a functional model practical for records classification. Existing models are complicated, lengthy, and too wordy and troublesome for records professionals to put into practice.

With that goal in mind, this book:

1. reviews case study at Department of Sariah Judiciary Malaysia (DSJM) to identify the records classification practice by public agencies in Malaysia;
2. reviews the existing classification models to learn the weaknesses and strength of those models;
3. provides a step-by-step approach to constructing and implementing records classification functional model.

ORGANIZATION OF THE TEXT

The text is organized into six chapters:

Chapter One: General Overview of Classification

The first chapter provides an overview of classification. Because of the nature of classification, which differs in its application in different facets of information management (the creative and the strategic information), it is important to understand the concept from various perspectives. Classification is central to categorizing information, including those embedded in records, into a systematic structure for control and retrieval purposes. It is a holistic concept and activity for information-related organizations to organize and manage information from the beginning of its creation to disposal. Classification from the records management perspective emphasizes the functions to ensure the contexts of records are intact and secured over time.

Chapter Two: What Is Classification?

This chapter reviews relevant and related concepts in defining records classification with the aim to provide critical appraisal of the past and the current thinking, and theories about classification. This chapter also covers classification from various perspectives, classification approaches, issues, and related past works on records classification. In records management field, classification is central to categorizing information including those embedded in records into a systematic structure for controlling and retrieval purposes. It is a holistic concept and activity for information-related organization to organize and manage information from the beginning of its creation to disposal. This chapter discusses the definition of concept related to classification; classification from various perspectives; and the classification based on human versus machine.

Chapter Three: Function-Based Classification

The chapter discusses the function-based classification, also referred to as records classification. Extensive coverage on the evolution of records classification in 17th century until 21st century onward involving various countries like Germany, France, Italy, England, and United States is discussed to show how the records classification has evolved and is important to employ. After proposing the records classification model, the authors have rigorously reviewed related past researches in records classification to identify the method employed and scope researched. Classification is becoming prevalent and gains its significance as more research was carried out, such as Orr (2005), Xie (2006), Ngoepe (2008), Foscarini (2009), Johare and Hussin (2010), and Krahn (2012). The research was focused on various aspects. For example, Ngoepe focused on records management, while Johare and Hussin focused on the functional requirements. However, both were referring to similar subject matter, the classification. It is, therefore; the authors would like to propose the integration of relevant theories to support the development of records classification system for government agencies.

Chapter Four: Records Management Models

Chapter four starts with a discussion on various classification models. The existing models are generic, normally represented in lengthy textual form, either with functional requirements or guidelines. These models are either functional or conceptual. Since records classification model is scarce, this chapter reviews the broader and more general records management models with the aim to forecast the inadequacy of existing classification models, which warrants a new model to be proposed.

Chapter Five: Records Classification Functional Model

The fifth chapter of this book covers the construction of the proposed records classification functional model. The new proposed model is represented in function modeling of records classification that includes all elements and activities occurred during classifying records. Also, classification models should include all elements related to classification including concepts and precepts of classification development, a plan or schema for implementation, and the way it is implemented or deployed. The function modeling is believed to enable the communication between IT and records management people.

Chapter Six: Conclusion

The sixth chapter concludes the discussion of records classification including analysis of current models and contributions of the proposed model. The proposed model would help organizations in creating their own classification system and also writing information-related policy. As classification can guarantee the continuity of business by ensuring vital records are kept safely, this chapter argues the importance and requirement for function-based classification for maintaining the integrity and authenticity of electronic records.

ACKNOWLEDGMENT

Classification is paramount to records management function. Although the concept is similar in meaning, it differs in its application in different fields. The model constructed in this book is a result of actual project work that is a product of countless hours spent in defining, visualizing, and validating the model. These efforts can only be performed in collaboration with knowledgeable, dedicated, and experienced practitioners and theorists. In particular, we would like to acknowledge the Department of Syariah Judiciary Malaysia and National Archives of Malaysia, for being cooperative whenever help was needed, colleagues and all of those who played an integral part in materializing this book.

The authors would like to thank the University Kebangsaan Malaysia and the Ministry of Science and Technology for the research grants.

CHAPTER ONE

General Overview of Classification

INTRODUCTION

Classification is a key foundational element of records management. It is used to systematize information and facilitate its retrieval. Classification is more established in library science than it is in records management. However, while the aim of both is to arrange and keep information systematically, the model is applied differently.

This entire aim of this book is to extensively discuss the classification in the records management context. It has been noted in this regard that the concept of classification is both understudied and not well understood. Research has shown that good records management strengthens government services by supporting business continuity; security and risk management; legal compliance and accountability; evidence-based decision making and transparency; good governance and public trust; good performance and government capability building (An, Shuyang, & Wei, 2011). Without proper understanding of such classification, it may be difficult or impossible to implement an efficient and effective records management initiative that addresses the complete life cycle of records from creation to preservation. Although classification plays a key role in the preservation of records over time, such systems may be overlooked or neglected when information systems are developed and implemented in favor of those elements of the records life cycle that focus on earlier stages such as storage and retrieval. Consequently, vast quantities of digital records have remained poorly managed over time.

CLASSIFICATION IN THE RECORDS MANAGEMENT CONTEXT

ISO 15489 has listed the processes of records management and determined how long it would take to retain, create, register, classify, store, control access, track, dispose off, and document the records management processes (ISO 15489, 2001). All the processes except for classification have not been given much consideration although many researchers have incorporated the

Records Classification: Concepts, Principles and Methods
ISBN 978-0-08-102238-2
http://dx.doi.org/10.1016/B978-0-08-102238-2.00001-9

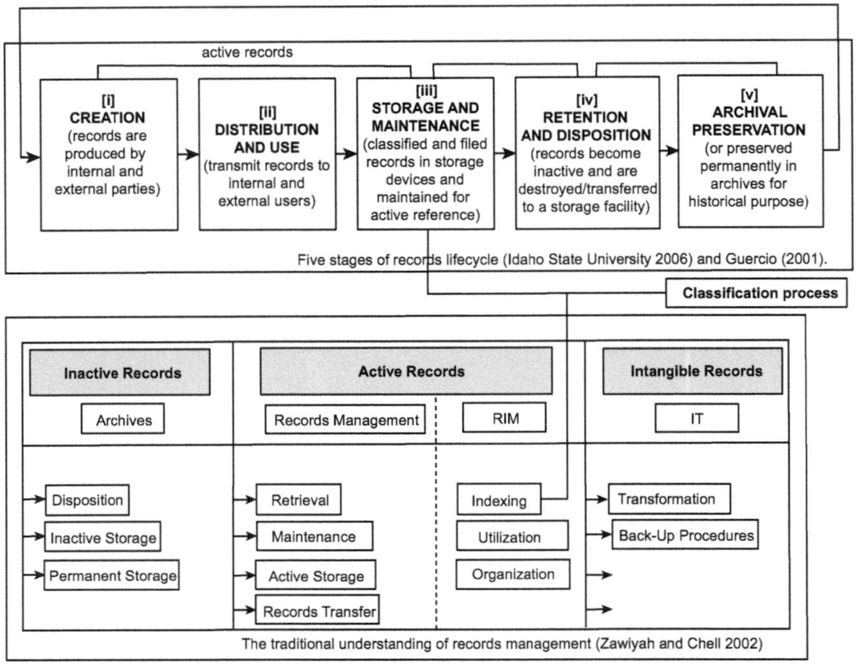

Figure 1.1 Classification based on the life-cycle phases of records. Modified from *Guercio, M. (May 6–8, 2001). Records classification and content management: Old functions and new requirements in the legislations and standards for electronic record-keeping system.* Proceedings of DLM-Forum 2002 access and preservation of electronic information: Best practices and solutions, Barcelona: 432–439. *Retrieved from* http://citeseerx.ist.psu.edu/viewdoc/downloaddoi=10.1.1.122.1484&rep=rep1&type=pdf#page=434; *Idaho State University. (2006).* Records and information management. *Retrieved from* http://www.isu.edu/infomgmt/program_scope.shtml; *Yusof, Z.M., & Chell, R.W. (2005).* Issues in records management. *Bangi: Penerbit UKM.*

concept into both the records life cycle and continuum models (Fig. 1.1). With the advances of information technology (IT), more and more (if not most) records are now created digitally or converted into digital format. Managing these records (electronic or digital) has become more challenging than the conventional ones.

Various tools have been developed to store and manage electronic records, with the aim of ensuring speedy retrieval. However, these tools have often been designed by IT professionals and implemented by organizations with little understanding of fundamental records management principles including the provenance of records classification techniques based on the functions and context of records; the life span of records governing their retention; and assessments of the value of records based on appraisal practices. These systematic techniques have been used for centuries in records systems (Guercio, 2001) and are applicable to electronic records.

Classification in records management shares similar concepts with other fields such as library and information science and IT but differs in its application. In library and information science, the purpose of classification is to classify creative information such as books to be accessed by users. It is defined by Maltby (1975) as "a systematic arrangement by subject of books and other material on shelves or of catalog entries in the manner which is most useful to those who read or who seek a definite piece of information." In IT, data are classified mainly for retrieval purposes. However, in records management, documents and records are systematically arranged for ultimate purpose of preservation. Moreover, records have evidentiary value, and losing them will put organizations at risk, and to retain this value, it is important to ensure the authenticity, reliability, integrity, and usability of records according to their business context in the organization (NARA, 2003).

When developing a system, IT professionals tend to focus on automating the creation and the management of active records with the aim of reducing space and to organize records, focusing more on system infrastructure matters such as protocol registers (a function used to identify and certify the existence and provenance of records) (Guercio, 2001; 2002). This has caused an imbalanced practice of excluding records management aspects while developing electronic system. To improve the situation, it is important for the IT and records management professionals to have balanced understanding and perception, and work hand in hand in designing the records management system (An et al., 2011). Furthermore, such collaboration is essential to produce reliable records from a systematic, complete, and supportive system that manages administrative and decision-making activities (Guercio, 2001). Many current electronic systems receive and store high volumes of data on a daily basis, but over time the quantity declines to minimum levels (RSD, n.d.). Documents that are declared as records, based on legal and retention requirements, are classified for longer retention and use, and these records are kept for future reference and evidence.

To qualify as evidence, records must be trustworthy (the concept is further depicted in Fig. 1.2) by maintaining the accuracy/originality (InterPARES1, 2002). Trustworthiness by definition is the quality of being dependable and reliable (Pearce-Moses, 2005). In the context of electronic records, trustworthiness implies that the system is dependable and produces consistent results based on established procedures. Records are trustworthy if they are accurate

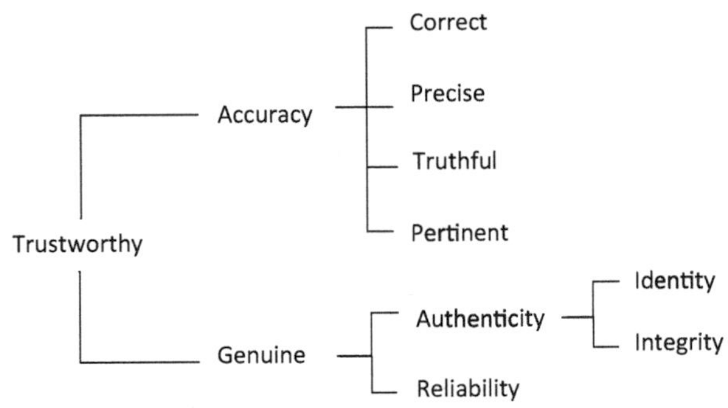

Figure 1.2 The concept of trustworthiness of records. Based on *InterPARES1. (2002).* Requirements for accessing and maintaining the authenticity for electronic records. *Retrieved from* http://www.interpares.org/book/interparesbookkapp02.pdf.

and genuine. The accuracy of records is the degree of precision to which records are correct, truthful, and free of error or distortion. Records are genuine or authentic if they are original (Garner, 2003). Authenticity is the quality of being genuine closely related with the creator of records, and could be maintained through its identity (creator) and integrity, which is the quality of being whole and unaltered. Reliability is the quality of being dependable and worthy of trust, which is able to produce consistent results, is created by competent authority according to established processes, and is complete in all format elements (Pearce-Moses, 2005). All these elements are related to each other to compose the concept of trustworthiness.

Not all documents are records, even though all records are documents. Documents consist of action, process, and a broader function of the records creator. On the other hand records consist of purpose, evidence, accountability, and memory creation and maintenance. However, both documents and records become virtual and destabilized in the electronic environment. Therefore, the management of both documents and records in an electronic environment requires far more significant actions and evidence throughout the records life cycle to determine their content and context (Cook, 2007).

One of the consequences of IT diffusion, through the massive use of personal computers and local area networks, the maturing of the internet, and the development of the World Wide Web and its enabling browser interface software, is the creation of electronic records in large volumes. These changes can be seen in the transformation of business functions, the way organizations and workers communicate, and the business records they create (Bantin, 2002). Communications have become less centralized and workplaces frequently virtual. Modern businesses processes have been significantly influenced by inter and intraorganizational information workflow and rapid transformations in the form of records such as hypermedia documents, dynamic documents, e-mails, and social media. This has led to records professionals debating about the theories, principles, and techniques that continue to guide them in their work. According to Cook (2007), new thinking and approaches are required for electronic records to reconceptualize traditional approaches, taking the best of these approaches and transforming them for the new age. Even so, the techniques and strategies of the custodial era, commonly applied during Jenkinson's time, are still relevant, there is a need to change and adopt new techniques and approaches as suggested in the post-custodial and postmodernist era.

THEORIES RELATED TO RECORDS MANAGEMENT

Records management was induced by two prominent theories in archival science: the Jenkinson and the Schellenberg. These two theories were devised for managing archival materials since both Jenkinson and Schellenberg are archivists though holding different schools of thoughts. While Jenkinson has greatly influenced the records management in the UK, Schellenberg has the same effect in the United States. Records management in the United States prefers the modern approach where selection and classification processes are paramount to control the volume of documents.

Records management is a process of managing records in accordance with policies, procedures, standards, best practices, and to comply with legislation. The initiative includes elements in the records management theory such as creation, use, dissemination, classification, retention schedules, appraisal, preservation, and disposition (ISO 15489). The general purpose of records management is to support the efficient continuation of records activities, ensuring evidence for internal purposes and regulatory compliance (Guercio, 2001). The relationship between records management and the efficiency of an organization's business activities needs to be identified and understood, because the control of the creation of records may not be effective if it is applied to an organization where functions and activities are not conducted efficiently (Guercio, 2001; Schellenberg, 1956).

Although records management is acknowledged as an academic field since 1970s, it lacks its own distinct theory (Finnell, 2011; Yusof & Chell, 2002). The field adapts theories and practices from other disciplines such as archival science, library science, information science, management, and law. According to Marcia (2006), records management is also known as document management for the purpose of keeping documents, with the ultimate aim of supporting heritage, historical and scientific research. Such an approach has been adopted by the UK government, and is thus known as a government approach (Millar, 2010), as established by Jenkinson (1965), In this approach, records must not be altered or destroyed as this can reduce their integrity and value as an impartial evidence of the past. Therefore, records and archives are considered to be synonymous in terms of definitions and use. Jenkinson asserts that no records should be disposed of, in order to protect their integrity, impartiality, authenticity, and archival value (Tschan, 2002). Therefore, the government approach adopted by European archival practice regards the duty of an archivist as of a passive custodian that keeps everything because archives are about custodial history, organic structure, and accumulation through natural process (Jenkinson, 1965; Tschan, 2002). Archives consist of interrelated records, and therefore the whole context about the records is required for preservation (Sutton, 1980). The effect of alteration and destruction of records may lead to a reduction in the integrity and value of records as an impartial evidence of the past.

In the United States, records are managed using business approach (Millar, 2010), pioneered by Schellenberg, to deal with the sheer volume of documents. US practice is less idealistic and more pragmatic interventionist based on a business approach. It was developed in response to requirements in the US environment to reduce bulk by selecting records that are permanently valuable among the masses of documentation, making this selection intelligently available to researchers. Thus, records and archives are different. Records are referred for active and semi-active phases, while archives, for non-active phases and normal use, are preserved in archives institution, based on their values (Schellenberg, 1956). In this model, records bear two values: primary (useful as evidence) and secondary (historical and cultural functions). The act of selection for permanent retention is based on an evaluation of secondary value, which is ultimately responsible for transforming records into archives (Tschan, 2002).

The differences between Schellenberg and Jenkinson arose through a need for a practical approach to deal with records. Records should not be altered or destroyed, their custody should be protected, and only the creator can destroy records (Jenkinson, 1965). Jenkinson recommends a "Golden Rule" to guide the selection process, and asserts that the administrator should ensure that the papers are in such a manner of "completeness and order." This indicates a requirement that everything an archivist would take into custody is well-ordered and "properly formed" archives, not masses of disorganized documentation. Such an approach was not popular in the United States as records are to be selected and classified to reduce volume, cut down organizational costs, and promote speedy retrieval (Tschan, 2002). Hence, only selected records with enduring value should be retained and preserved (Schellenberg, 1956). This principle of *respect des fonds* is still upheld based on the belief that archives are created in the course of activities to accomplish specific purposes. Therefore, records must be kept without mutilation, alteration, or unauthorized destruction.

Records management theory gained importance as a consequence of Schellenberg's practice in the early 1900s, with an increased focus on the life cycle of records that had previously been limited to only three stages (Charman, 1984; Hardcastle, 1989). As records management progressed, both as a career and academic field, the concept of a life cycle evolved and its various components multiplied. It now includes activities such as declaration as records, moving content to enterprise archives, placing records on litigation hold, releasing legal holds on records, making records anonymous, declassifying records, and disposing of records (RSD, n.d.). Records management now deals with more complex phases in relation to its life cycle and authenticity challenges due to the pervasiveness of electronic records in government. Efficient and effective records management initiatives are often a high priority particularly in developing countries (Yaacob & Sabai, 2011). Poor records management systems are a major barrier to institutional, legal, and regulatory reforms; anticorruption strategies; and poverty reduction and economic development (Lipchak & McDonald, 2003). Records management also promotes accountability, transparency, and trust (Mnjama & Wamukoya, 2007; Wamukoya & Mutula, 2005).

Theoretical Framework

According to Dissertation-help.co (1999), a theoretical framework is "a sensible collection of interrelated concepts just like a proposed theory to determine a roadmap to the research work for getting better and accurate results, the measures, the objects, and the statistical relationships that a researcher should look for." It is a theory-testing sort of a model. Therefore, the theories proposed must be well-thought out. Theoretical frameworks are important for every range of research but particularly so for explanatory research work, where the researcher really does not know what is going on and where the research would take him or her.

The three components that make up the theoretical framework of this study include the concepts, principles, and methods of archival science, library and information science, and management science each of which impacts the classification of records. These elements, including the ideas relevant to functional analysis for purposes of classification that records keepers have been dwelling upon over the last few decades, are further discussed in Chapter 2.

The first component is archival science, which has been radically reconceived by recognizing its subjective nature. Archival science is characterized as objective (such as the matter, the recorded product, the information system), neutral, impersonal, and disinterested (Kuhn, 1962). Archival science theory entails custody, impartiality, *respect des fonds*, and the principle of provenance. The theory of classification may not have been fully articulated by the archival scholars and practitioners, yet, as Livelton (1996) observed, methods to organize records in the current phase of their continuum have nonetheless been developed and used. More specifically, the functional approach as a classification method seems to be considered suited to the nature of records and the purposes of classification by those who have been devising such means. In an analysis of various theoretical works on the subject, as well as the discourse about methods (Eastwood, 2007), one would expect to find some enduring ideas about the purpose of classification, the meaning of function, as well as the nature and characteristics of the material being classified.

Archival science theory, however, has been disputed by new science that is based on the process where the contextual dependence of the whole is more important than the autonomy of the parts. The new theory known as postmodern does not disclaim archival principles, but rather changes them from being a product-focused to a process-oriented activity, from custody to post-custody (Jenkinsonian guardianship of evidence from physical records to a conceptual framework) (MacNeil, 1994). The term post-custodial means that the archival practices or mindsets formed in the older custodial era of paper records, i.e., older perceptions of records creation and records management must change (Cook, 2007). This change is enhanced by a focus on the context, purpose, intent, interrelationships, functionality, and accountability of the records and creator, and processes involved in creation. This is deemed crucial in the electronic world where records are no longer tangible, but more fluid and virtual, a world where it has become difficult to trace the custody of records. The post-custodial idea is supported by many influential worldwide archivists such as David Bearman, Margaret Hedstrom, Helen Samuel, and Charles Dollar (United States), Hugh Taylor and Terry Cook (Canada), Angelica Menne-Haritz (Germany), Glenda Acland, Sue McKemmish, Frank Upward, and Peter Scott (Australia).

Archival principles are still useful when it comes to the context of records. The context of records safeguards their integrity and authenticity. This is provenance. However, a slight difference has transpired between three specific properties of paper and electronic records, that is, their content, context, and structure. These differences are most apparent in the context of records, an important element because, without it, information, data, or documents are not regarded as records that can act as good corporate memory and are accountable (Cook, 2007). In the electronic world, an understanding of the conceptual context, business process, and functional purpose behind the creation of a record is crucial. The context of an organization's functions, business processes, work cycles, and transactions within the functional process matrix needs to be captured in system designs to distinguish information from records and to preserve records as the most vital evidence of important transactions, activities, and functions. All of these prescriptions are vital to ensure the integrity and accountability of electronic records.

Duranti (1998) asserts that records management and diplomatics are inextricably linked, especially when dealing with classification, routing, forms, and the genesis of records. Diplomatics establishes rules to examine the value of documents including the through study of the genesis of documentation, analysis, inner constitutions, and transmissions of documents, and the relationships between facts and creators. This approach can be adopted to ascertain the provenance, and determine the authenticity of records, both of which are crucial in determining the context of records in the electronic world.

The second component of the framework is library and information science (first component is archival science). Budd (1995) states that the reason and core of a library's existence is "to collect, organize and provide access to information." However, this statement contains two different notions, namely:

1. the process of collecting, storing, and retrieving, and
2. the object of the process, namely information (Mai, 2004). Thus, classification in librarianship qualifies as a practical, retrieval-oriented technique that has nothing of the necessary-ness, or determined nature that characterizes the archival concept of classification. This makes the design

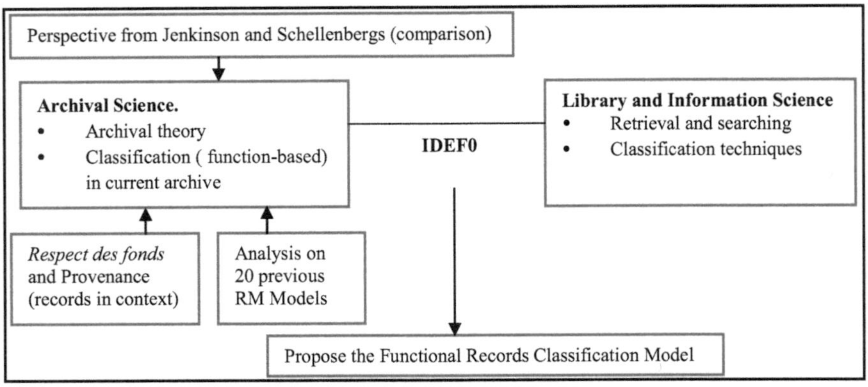

Figure 1.3 Theoretical framework.

of classification models definitely more straightforward in a library than it could ever be in an archive (Foscarini, 2009).

The third component is the development of records classification model. The process is achieved through a method known as IDEF0 (ICAM definition for function modeling, where ICAM is an acronym for Integrated Computer-Aided Manufacturing). IDEF0 is a design tool to draw the model and has been adopted in previous research by Presley, Sarkis, and Liles (1997), Presley, Sarkis, and Liles (2000), and Perumpalath (2005). The theoretical framework is depicted in Fig. 1.3.

These authors have adopted a combination of theories from archival science, and library and information science. The contribution of archival theory is the examination of records both extrinsically and intrinsically, an important factor in the process of classifying records. The contribution of library and information science in general, and specifically from an IT perspective, is to view records through their evolution from machine readable, then electronic, to digital (Cook, 1992). This evolution of records has resulted in changes in traditional archival theory, from one that previously dealt mostly with paper/physical records, into modern practices, which have been widely adopted in United States, Australia, and a few European countries. These changes can be seen in references in archival theory to a paradigm shift, or a new formulation (Cook, 1997, 2001) especially in methodologies of functional analysis, appraisal, and job scopes. Duranti (1998), on the other hand, asserts that the concept of provenance in archival theory is still useful when dealing with records context, which is also included in this book.

This study proposes a records classification model for Malaysia that is based on a functional analysis of organization's activities, using the IEDF0 method. A review of existing models, including functional requirements as a statement of a function required by a system (Underwood, 1997), was conducted to develop the proposed model. Functional model for records classification is developed using the IDEF0 notation to depict the highest to lowest level of classification for the purpose of establishing or improving communication between records management and IT professionals.

RECORDS MANAGEMENT AND E-GOVERNMENT INITIATIVE

The introduction of electronic government (e-government) initiative in Malaysia has made records management inevitable for good governance (Palvia & Sharma, 2007). The e-government system has the ability to transform relations with citizens, businesses, and government that can serve to a variety of ends; better delivery service to citizens; improved interactions; citizen empowerment; more efficient government that provides benefits with less corruption; increased transparency; greater convenience; revenue growth; and cost reduction (World Bank, 2005). With an understanding of the potential benefits of e-government, the government of Malaysia embarked on the initiative but has encountered a range of issues and potential impediments (Nawi, Rahman, & Ibrahim, 2005; Ramli, 2012), mainly because it focuses on technology to deliver an online transactions platform.

Malaysia, along with other countries such as the United States, the UK, and the Republic of Korea (to name a few), has experienced the transition from paper-based government to an electronic one with the aim of achieving a paperless office environment. This change has affected government agencies and the work environment administratively. Although staff seemed ready to embrace the change from manual to electronic systems (Mokhtar & Yusof, 2009), many have yet to achieve good results, especially in the implementation of records management initiative and systems (Yusof, 2009). In other words, although records management is essential for government and public institutions at all stages of development (Yaacob & Sabai, 2011), the processes of automating administrative work and managing records electronically based on records management principles are still not given high priority (Mokhtar & Yusof, 2009). Consequently, a major barrier exists for institutional, regulatory reform, anticorruption strategies, poverty reduction, and economic development (Lipchak & McDonald, 2003).

Unlike developed countries, which have extended their attention to information and records in business systems (Heeks, 1999), the Malaysian government has focused solely on the technological aspects of systems making it the core element in an e-government initiative (Zouridis & Thaens, 2003). This attention to technology has, in turn, created a range of issues and impediments (Nawi et al., 2005; Ramli, 2012). The imbalance of attention between the records and IT aspects of e-government has resulted in 35% in total project or implementation failures, and 50% in partial failures (Heeks, 2003). The initiative is lagging behind time and has failed to deliver the expected benefits (Lipchak & McDonald, 2003; Nawi et al., 2005).

The e-government initiative does not only involve information communication and technology (ICT) supporting government operations and services, but has also been used to transform processes in which public services are generated and delivered (Palvia & Sharma, 2007). An e-government implementation relies on government records that contain evidence, rights, and responsibilities of government, and are a source of public accountability and mandates of citizens (Piggot, 2002). Without access to such records, ad hoc decisions may be carried out arbitrarily without considering their benefits to the institutional memory. This in turn, would place an organization at risk.

In Malaysia, the implementation of e-government initiatives has grown from being simply the provision of infrastructure and human skills to user-centric approaches on government websites and systems (Ismail, 2010). However, the expected benefits are yet to be realized. In 2009, statistics from the Public Complaints Bureau listed 10 complaints pertaining to poor public service delivery, including 46.6% relating to "late/no action/feedback," clearly implying a lack of information or difficulties in retrieving documents or other information quickly (Ismail, 2010). In 2010, Malaysia's rank as an e-government leader dropped to the 32nd before further declining to the 40th spot in 2012 (United Nations, 2012).

E-government constitutes a major subset of government (Palvia & Sharma, 2007) that should be underpinned by good records management in order to provide good governance with transparency, accountability, and trust (Lipchak, 2002; Mnjama & Wamukoya, 2007). Hence, there is a crucial need to explore the relationship between records management and good governance as this may contribute to the success or failure of e-government initiatives.

The classification of records supports better service delivery. In 2007, the government of Malaysia confirmed the importance of developing classification systems as well as retention schedules before implementing an electronic records management system by the year 2014 (Service Circular, 2007). Since classification systems do not exist in government agencies, initiatives to develop them are subjected to the availability of experts to complete the work required. In reality, records classification has rarely been considered and the role of records management professionals in developing systems for information retrieval is not widely recognized (Milne, 2009). As reported by Johare and Hussin (2010), the need to be able to classify records in records management systems (ICA 2008a, 2008b, 2008c; InterPARES1, 2002; MoReq2, 2008; National Archives of Australia, 2008; National Archives of Malaysia, 2008; UK Public Record Office, 2002) constituted less than 10% of all requirements, compared to the requirements for other processes such as retention, disposal, capture, and the ability to manage authentic and reliable records.

The situation is considered to be even more serious when it is realized that information (including records) is not featured in the Malaysian National Information Policy. E-government in Malaysia is more focused on technology than the information used by or stored in those technology solutions, under the belief that the former can overcome issues related to the latter. According to the National Information Technology Agenda (1996), Malaysia has embraced e-government ideas and implemented projects based on the utilization of ICT with the aim of producing a knowledge-based society and economy by the year 2020. Despite the obvious highlighting of the knowledge needed to achieve this goal, Malaysian national policy does not address the need for effective records management or the importance of managing information, which in turn has led to the failure of some e-government projects (NITA, 1996). This lack of focus led to a lack of awareness among civil servants about records management. The absence of records management elements, including computerized classification, is attributed to the Malaysian emphasis on technology (ICT).

WHY DOES CLASSIFICATION MATTER?

Research on classification in records management is scarce, even less so in relation to function-based classification (or also known as records classification) (Orr, 2005). Most research emphasizes on the aspect of standards and guidelines; technological issues; appraisal, and preservation. Classification from a records management perspective is not given attention and is rarely discussed; studies are more isolated (Feng, An, Liu, & Dawson, 2009; Orr, 2005; Xie, 2008) and under-researched (Mokhtar & Yusof, 2015; Santangelo, 2009) since its application is wrongly perceived as being only appropriate and applicable to the library context. Furthermore, the absence of a theory of classification also contributes to the problem, as most or all studies in classification were largely undertaken by the library and information science (Jones, 2005; Szostak, 2004). In the library and information science field, classification was developed relatively arbitrarily because of lack of a consistent theoretical background and methodology (Alberts, Schellinck, Eby, & Marleau, 2010), which in turn affected the usability of systems (Orr, 2005). The application of classification differs between the library and records management fields. In the library field, classification is used for retrieval and searching (Ariff, 2008; Evans, 2007), whereas in records management, classification is designed to be used for preservation purposes and to maintain required records characteristics (Schellenberg, 1956). The authenticity, reliability, integrity, and usability of records must be maintained throughout the life cycle.

Initiatives have been undertaken to provide guidelines for developing records classification systems (Foscarini, 2009; Krahn, 2012). Most of the initiatives can be found in standards, guidelines, principles, functional requirements, or handbook form. These are usually qualitative models made up of conceptual models that come in many styles, and emphasize the ability to assist records manager, archivists, or researchers. Conceptual models could be used as a foundation in the development of more complex systems (Carleton College, 2009).

In Malaysia, function-based classification for electronic records is still absent despite the requirement for it in records management initiatives. E-SPARK (*Elektronik Sistem Pemeliharaan Arkib Rekod Kerajaan*) project was launched in 2008 to guide governments for developing electronic systems, without highlighting on the classification issue. Whereas, most existing international models provide functional requirements to develop electronic systems for the management of records from creation to preservation such as ISO 16175 (2011), MoReq (2001), MoReq2 (2008), Moreq2010 (2011), and ICA (2008a, 2008b, 2008c).

It is evident that managing electronic records is becoming central, and hence it is crucial to manage these records. However, there are issues identified such as the absence of theory of classification, the needs for classification are not well articulated in the current functional requirements, and the concept of classification is not well understood. These issues have however became the motivation to embark on this study with the main intention to propose a model for electronic records classification based on its functions.

A classification model is crucial to guide the development of a function-based classification system in organizations as it can show the functionality of a system and the logical interconnections between functions (Burge, 2011) that focus on the classification process. The model also describes how classification flows operate from the highest level with a view of the overall system, decomposed down to lower levels, describing the detailed component specifications (Muller, 2007).

The approach used to describe the classification process can be a way for the users in different fields to communicate by connecting the system design and description from upper to lower level. This is the basis of the proposed model to represent knowledge about function-based classification and to communicate with users from different interrelated fields. This is parallel with current trends of electronic records management especially in e-government, which moves toward multidisciplinary and collaborative approaches to manage records as information resources and business assets (An et al., 2011).

This book is based on a research, which adopts qualitative methods of inquiry. In a qualitative study, inquirers state research questions or hypotheses, but not a research objectives as in a quantitative study and research questions are as broad as possible. The question "How was a classification system designed?" was always kept at the forefront while researching into the concept and the application of classification into practice, particularly in records management.

Two broad categories of subjects potentially sharing different views on the topics under examination were identified, namely the system "developers" and the system "users." The system "developers" could be archivist, records managers, members of project teams, or anyone entrusted with the task of designing, maintaining, and/or implementing the records classification system in use, in the organization. On the other hand, the system "users" could be both ordinary and specialized users of records classification systems including among the first groups, area managers, experts, secretaries; and among the second group, system administrators, records manager who are not involved in the development of the system. Taking this into consideration, and with the purpose of breaking the issue down to fragment the major question into more manageable units, the following more specific questions, are elaborated.

1. Are developers aware of the existing classification (if there is any) and what are their opinions about it?
2. In developing the system, what approach is favored (either function or subject-based)?

3. Are developers aware that records classification system is commonly designed either as function or subject-based?
4. What influenced the developers to determine the choice of either function or subject-based system?
5. With particular reference to electronic legal records, are developers aware of specific requirements for the design of classification system for electronic legal records?
6. Is the requirement for records management always taken into consideration or is it a purely technical requirement (IT)?
7. Are developers aware that the requirement for classification of records is different from both the records management and IT perspectives?
8. Are developers aware that records have life cycles, which begin with creation and end with disposal?
9. Why are records managers not involved, or not participate in the design stage of system?
10. Are developers aware that the design of current classification system is limited only to storage and retrieval purposes?

As the aim of this book is to propose a new functional records classification model for managing electronic records in the public agencies particularly in Malaysia, therefore, prior to developing the model, it is deemed necessary to critically review the existing records classification models to assess both the drawbacks and the strengths of those models. This helps to justify why the new records classification model is required. Therefore, the author had to assess first the current classification system in Malaysia and second the previous function-based classification models.

This book focuses mainly on developing a functional records classification model for managing electronic records in public agencies in Malaysia, with Syariah court records serving as the case study. The Department of Syariah Judiciary Malaysia was selected because the Malaysian government has urged the agencies to use computerized systems to overcome problems of delays in making court decisions accessible, which shows how the limitation of system's functions, which is only to computerize the workflow process without considering the requirement for a classification function for records.

Classification becomes the focus of this study because it could contribute to the preservation of records for future reference, evidence, memories, and research. Without classification, organizations could be at risk. The other elements in the records life cycle are not covered, since much has already been written about them.

This work is significant in the sense to convey the importance of the problem for different groups that may profit from reading and using the study (Creswell, 2009). This would provide a better understanding of the issues involved in managing electronic records by public organization in Malaysia, particularly in the midst of e-government initiatives. The model would provide a form of advisory service to government organizations. The electronic records management specification developed by e-SPARK has been simplified for system development throughout the records life cycle, with no specification included for classification purposes. Therefore, classification for electronic records is important as its absence could lead to unsystematic management, which in turn may eventually put organizations at risk of losing records. As evidenced in developed countries, internally generated, well-managed records can underline the difference between weak and strong, sustainable and competitive, organizations. This study also highlights the records management field as crucial in managing information especially in the information society and with so many knowledge-based activities. Hence, records and information not only become the concern of technology because technology is a medium used to convey the message and act as a tool, but are the core elements for management, systems, and processes. The information provided would benefit records managers, organizations, researchers, information professionals, and the field of records management will benefit from having a new model specifically designed for classification purposes.

CONCLUSION

Records are important for their values in providing evidence and heritage. Records can be considered valuable and worthy if they are authentic, reliable, usable, and have integrity. Because records are a product of actions, it is crucial to provide a classification model that is based on functions of records so that the action involved in creating records remains intact and trustworthy, and to ensure that classified records are reliable. Classification processes are required at active phases of a record's life cycle to ensure that records are arranged systematically in context and to maintain their integrity and trustworthiness. It is also crucial to undergo a classification process as, without it, a records management initiative is incomplete and puts organizations at risk because valuable and vital records could be destroyed prematurely or unintentionally. Valueless records may also be kept longer than the required period which would increase operating cost, timely information retrieval may be deterred, and it may not be possible to locate and produce relevant records when they are needed.

Furthermore, records classification is still scarcely researched worldwide, and is under-researched in Malaysia. Classification is commonly associated with library and information science, one that focuses on searching and retrieval functions. The absence of records classification in Malaysia is one of the outcomes from present-day scenarios that focus more on searching and retrieving function to the detriment of records management, subsequently putting organizations at risk. The commencement of e-government has underscored the need for records classification, as records management is essential for government to provide high-quality information to enable the government to make decisions and take actions to improve economic development, ensure justice, protect the environment, provide security and achieve other governance objectives (Lipchak & McDonald, 2003). Therefore, this study was undertaken to propose a new records classification model, one that will then act as a foundation and reference to develop the classification system in Malaysia. This model focuses on the functions involved and represents the function modeling to assist developers, records managers, professionals, and scholars in developing the system.

CHAPTER TWO

What Is Classification?

INTRODUCTION

In records management field, classification is central to categorizing information, including that embedded in records, into a systematic structure for controlling and retrieving purposes. It is a holistic concept and activity for information-related organization to organize and manage information from the beginning of its creation to disposal. The classification from records management perspective emphasizes the functions to ensure the context of records is intact and secured over time.

The chapter discusses the definition of concept related to classification: the evolution of electronic records, differences between electronic and paper records, classification from various perspectives, and classification by human and machine.

CONCEPTS RELATED TO CLASSIFICATION

Defining concepts is essential to increase the body of knowledge regarding the topic discussed. By doing so would reduce confusions and misunderstandings because different bodies of knowledge about any topic have different defined concepts related to the topic (Botsch, 2011). In this chapter, various concepts related to classification are discussed such as information, document, records, life cycle, and the term classification itself. These terms must be explained as some authors use them interchangeably while others strictly differentiate the meaning. Only by understanding the terms, one could understand why classification for information, in general, differs from classification for records, in specific.

Although records are commonly discussed, different fields perceived the concept differently. People commonly understand that records are similar to documents, information, or data. The appropriate understanding of record is essential since data, information, and documents are not necessarily records. This misunderstanding can influence the efficiency and effectiveness of managing records. The incorrect understanding of the meaning of records will

Records Classification: Concepts, Principles and Methods
ISBN 978-0-08-102238-2
http://dx.doi.org/10.1016/B978-0-08-102238-2.00002-0

not only hamper in executing the initiative but can also put organization at risk. Therefore, this section defines the concepts used in this book to better understand the context of classification in records management field.

Information

The terms information, document, and records are commonly used alternately. However, each has its own definition and concept. According to Buckland (1991) and Budd (2011) there are three types of information: "as-process," "as-knowledge," and "as-thing." Information "as-process" happens when someone is informed or has received information, what someone knows has changed. Information "as-knowledge" is information to denote what is perceived in information "as-process."The third type of information "as-thing" is also used for objects such as data and documents that are also referred to as information because they are regarded as being informative.

Like records, information also has value but the value of information is not quantifiable; it depends on content and use. The value of information is an individual determination; that is, information that may have value for one person may not have any value for another. Information is also a dynamic force for change in the systems within which it operates; it must be viewed within an organization as a formative organizational entity rather than as an accumulated stockpile of facts (Eaton & Bawden, 1991).

Document

A document is defined as any written or printed work; a writing, or printed work of legal or official nature that may be used as evidence or proof as record. Documents may be information or data fixed in some media and, if it is not part of the official records, it is a non-record (Pearce-Moses, 2005). Document was traditionally considered as text fixed on paper (Lysakowski, 1997). However, the tradition has changed and now it includes all media and formats. Photographs, drawings, sound recordings and videos, word processing files, spreadsheets, web pages, and databases reports are now generally considered to be documents (ANSI/NISO, 2003).

Like records, document is traditionally understood to have content, context, and structure. However, the nature of these attributes may change in electronic documents. Electronic formats could present information in complex layers that are three-dimensional or have a nonlinear structure. The phrase "four-corner document" is sometimes used to distinguish an electronic document that could be printed on paper without loss of information from a more complex, three-dimensional document. Similarly, some electronic document content is not fixed, but may change over time, for example, a word processing document that pulls data from a constantly changing database. These documents are described as dynamic documents to distinguish from traditional, fixed documents (Pearce-Moses, 2005).

Document differs from records in some contexts when it refers to an item that is not a record (InterPARES2, 2008); for example, drafts, duplicates of record copies, and materials are not directly related to business activities. In this sense, document is not usually included in retention schedules and could be disposed of without authorization. However, in other contexts, a document can be used synonymously with a record. "Records" in this sense connotes an official document, especially the final version of one created in the routine course of business with the specific purpose of keeping information for later use as evidence or proof of the thing to which it refers.

The term "document" will be used consistently in the section below because records may include documents, although not all documents are records. The differences between documents and records (or archives) were justified by Jenkinson (1937), where all manuscripts, regardless of materials of make, are documents, while records/archives are the ones produced by administrative transactions and subsequently kept for short or long term, or forever. In the modern world, the best approach to understand a document is to examine what information is readily available to the computer user in the ordinary course of business; if the employee can view the information, it should be treated as the equivalent of a paper "document" (Sedona Principles, 2003).

On the other hand, data that can be readily compiled into information, whether presented on the screen or printed on paper, is also a "document" under Rule 34 (Sedona Principles, 2003). However, data that is used by a computer system but is hidden and never revealed to the user in the ordinary course of business should not be presumptively treated as a "document," nor should the data that is not accessible except through forensic means, such as deleted or residual data.

Records

Records are defined as a written or printed work of a legal or official nature that may be used as evidence or proof of something: a document; data or information that has been fixed on some medium: that has content, context, and structure and is used as an extension of human memory or to demonstrate accountability; data or information in a fixed form that is created or received in the course of individual or institutional activity and set aside (preserved) as evidence of that activity for future reference; any instrument filed for public notice (constructive notice), a phonograph record; and any computing of related data elements treated as a unit, such as the fields in a row in a database table or description of entry describing a work in a catalog (Pearce-Moses, 2005).

The term "record" is relatively generic and cannot be used to explain or provide evidence of a specific activity. For example, records created through administrative processes are often called administrative records, and the list goes on—the word "records" may be prefixed with words such as accession, agency aggregated, architectural, archival, associated, business, catalog, content, contingent, conventional, corporate, current, dispositive, electronic, emergency-operating, engineering-essential, facilitative, frozen, graphic, housekeeping, important, inactive; input, local, memorial, municipal, narrative, noncurrent, non-textual, notarial, official, operational, organizational, permanent, presidential, printed, probative, program, public, semicurrent, special, structure, supporting, temporary, textual, transitory, and vital.

The Malaysian National Archive Act (2003) provides the basis for the Electronic Records Management and Archive Policy, and defined records as "materials in written or other form stating the facts or events or otherwise recording information that includes papers, documents, registers, printed materials, books, maps, plans, drawings, photographs, cinematograph films, sound recordings, produced records regardless of electronic or physical characteristics and any copy thereof."

A record has fixed content, context, and structure (ANSI/NISO 2003; Lysakowski, 1997). Content is the text, data, symbol, numeral, image, sound, graphic, and other information that makes up the substance of the records. The ability of a record to "fix" the substance of the information so that it can be repeated, recited, or recalled at a later date means that it functions as an extension of memory; this is at the heart of the concept of record. A record may be created specifically to preserve information over time or to prevent future misinterpretation of that information, although a record could not be presumed to be reliable without some form of authentication. However, any item, no matter how ephemeral it was originally intended to be, may serve as a record if it is later used as evidence of the thing to which it refers.

Fixity is the quality of content being stable and resisting change. To preserve memory effectively, the content of a record must be consistent over time. Records made on mutable media, such as electronic records, must be managed so that it is possible to demonstrate that the content has not degraded or been altered. A record may be fixed without being static. A computer program may allow a user to analyze and view data in many different ways. A database itself may be considered a record if the underlying data is fixed and the same analysis and resulting view remain the same over time.

Context is the organizational, functional, and operational circumstances surrounding the creation, receipt, storage, or use of a record. Context includes the date and place when the record was created, compiled, or issued, and its relationship with other records. It must be possible to ascertain how a record relates to other records and to the organization that created it (Jisc Infonet, 2012).

Structure refers to the physical characteristics of a record and the internal organization of its contents. Record structure is the form that makes the content tangible and intelligible. Physical characteristics include components and methods of assembly, such as paper, ink, seals, and font families, or character sets, encoding, and file formats. Structure also includes the intellectual organization of a document. The structure of a record may be simple, such as plain text on a page; it may be organized into an outline or sections with headings; or it may be highly complex, including a preamble, the body, and the signature of witnesses.

The structure of a document is contained within boundaries that define a record as a unit and give it identity by distinguishing it from other information. A record may consist of many physically or logically discrete parts that function together as unit, such as several pages or data values from many tables, but these parts must be bound together in some fashion.

Records connote documents rather than artifacts or published materials, although collections of records may include artifacts and books. Records are defined in terms of their function rather than their characteristics; the definition is extended to include many materials not normally considered to be a record. For example, an artifact may function as a record even though it falls outside the vernacular understanding of the definition.

In this book, the discussion relates specifically to electronic and current records. Electronic records are any information that is recorded in a form that only a computer can process and that satisfies the definition of a record. The electronic records could be from databases, spreadsheets, electronic mail (email), offline or online systems, and any electronic medium that can create or store content, such as smartphones, machines, and gadgets (Pearce-Moses, 2005). In this book, the term records are used interchangeably with electronic records. Both the terms carry similar meaning, i.e., electronic records.

Electronic Records

Records in the electronic environment have evolved from being machine-readable record into electronic and digital records (Cook, 2001).

Machine-readable records are the first generation in the 1960–1970s. Records produced in this era were used as the basis for more substantive paper records. These records consisted of a fixed output resulting from a single input, and a series of computational processes typically took the form of punch cards, printout reports, statistical tables, or visual displays which were used as source or supporting information in traditional documentary records (physical or paper). From this early effort to appraise machine-readable records, valuable insight was gained to differentiate between data, and records (Krahn, 2012). Data is considered to be information content but that lacks of structure and context required to generate a meaningful records activity, whereas records included the context of creation and use, corresponding to organizational structure, and arrangement, thereby providing essential evidential value (Pearce-Moses, 2005). The distinction of data and records became fundamental to the latter responses in the sense of intellectual, strategic, technical, and legal of archival profession in relation to computer-generated information (Krahn, 2012).

Electronic records were conceded in 1980–1990s, consisted of contextual support due to succeeded varying software development that was dynamic and relational. The development of dynamic and relational software was in response to the emergence of hierarchical networked and particularly relational database as well as personal computers becoming pervasive in the modern workplace. However, the early electronic records were unstructured, virtual, fleeting, and devoid of context, and were made up of different textual, audio, and graphical components. Moreover, the output of these records could be found stored on countless digital media types. Consequently, these records became impossible to trace due to diversity of form that not only was content not tied to its relational context but also the records could not be removed from the technological context of creation and use, without losing records meaning.

Digital record became known in 2000s. These records were built on the work of the electronic records by widening its scope and complexity to deal with the exponential growth of computerized records and the changing focus of computer uses.

Life Cycle

A life cycle describes the distinct phases of a record's existence, from creation to final disposition. The life cycle model for managing records by Schellenberg and others is the prominent model for North American archivists and record managers since at least the 1960s (Pearce-Moses, 2005). The model for paper and electronic records are portrayed differently because of their distinct characteristics (Yusof & Chell, 2000), because the life cycle for paper records differs from the records continuum of electronic records. The life cycle of paper records has three distinct stages: active; semi-active; and non-active. The last stage usually includes the destruction of a record or its surrender to archives after a predefined period (Yusof & Chell, 2005). The continuum is a map of dynamic, virtual places of logical entities that is drawn both holistically and multidimensionally. The records continuum defines the stages from the creation of a record to its reuse, a cycle with four dimensions and four vectors: recordkeeping; authority; transactional; and evidentiality. These four vectors interact to achieve a continuous and dynamic whole, which ranges over four dimensions: document accountable acts, capture records, organize recordkeeping regime, and ensure societal memory (Upward, 1998, pp. 110–130). The continuum of records is nothing new. In the 1980s, Jay Atherton once gave a thought on records life cycle to continuum, and has been explained considerably by Frank Upward, Sue Mckemmish, and Barbara Reed (to name a few).

Classification

Classification is a management tool that provides for a systematic arrangement of objects into groups or categories (Chosky, 2006; Franks, 2013; Guercio, 2002; Xie, 2006), and is commonly used for systematic identification and arrangement of business activities and/or records into categories according to logically structured conventions, methods, and procedural rules as represented in a classification system (ISO 15489-1, 2001). In business, classification is a process that helps an organization describe, organize, and control information that builds upon an analysis of the organization's business activities.

The terms "classification" and "arrangement" were used synonymously in Schellenberg's modern archives approach without confronting extensively on the complexities of classification. On the other hand, Jenkinson's manual discussed the topic appropriately in different terms such as "differentiation" and the "placing" of records (MacLean, 1956; Schellenberg, 1961). The use of the classification and arrangement terminology has narrowed the implementation of both, as arrangement has been defined as a process that reflected inventory processes, using terms such as "groups," "sub-groups," "series," and "items," while the terms "placement" and "differentiation" have been used less often.

Classification based on functions and activities has been preferred for controlling information and records, and is based on classifying records according to why records exist, rather than record topic. That is, it focuses on the context and use of records, rather than their content. A function-based classification system benefits organizations because it provides the following: an understanding of the relationship between the business and its records; identification of records required for their evidential value; prioritization of records for business value; and facilitation of retention decisions. The classification of records is a holistic concept based on the functions of an organization. A records classification scheme, also known as a file plan, is a process that may be used to categorize or group records into retrieval units. A file plan used to classify records based on business activities that generate records, and derives directly from an organization's business classification scheme. It is typically represented as a directory or folder structure such as function→activity→topic→subtopic (Franks, 2013).

Most studies tend to emphasize the technological aspects of classification; particularly how to automate classification, even though a theory of classification is yet to be developed (Hjørland & Pedersen, 2005). Records management specialists are driven by time and space to study many subjects, but generally they do not closely examine classification, because library and information science and computer specialists have deliberately monopolized the area. The lack of research on classification from a records management perspective has impacted the related literature, the manual or automatic development of classification systems, and the implementation of classification schemes. This is due to a number of factors including the following: complexity of defining record characteristics; a thorough preliminary study of organizations; and detailed documentary analysis to ensure that records are correctly selected and classified. These processes are tedious, and records management researchers need to conduct further studies in this area. Most records management professionals have examined other areas, such as appraisal, preservation, or standards (Hjørland, 2008; Mai, 2004; Xie, 2008).

Classification is made up of several related principles including access, retrieval, maintenance, retention, and disposal. A classification system should be based on the size and volume of a company and the volume of its records, how and by whom records are used, and how quickly records could be accessed (Schellenberg, 1956; Wallace, 1987). Classification systems allow records to be accessed easily, with the ability to retrieve all records including annotations and attachments, in the context of which the records belong. These systems also allow records to be maintained in their own context throughout the life cycle, and preserved or destroyed based on classification comprehensive retention schedules that provide either control over preservation and custody or justification for the destruction of records (MacNeil, 2002).

The application of classification differs among various groups within the information management community, namely librarians, archivists, records managers, and information technology people. For example, librarians classify content based on subjects and this works well with discrete or standalone items such as books or maps (Xie, 2007). IT professionals, on the other hand, classify documents by building models that can correctly predict the class of different objects; this in turn assists in allowing organizations to systematically organize, access, and process documents (Ab. Aziz, 2004). Classification may also be associated with the categorization of records and documents based on the degree of secrecy and functionality of records. This study adopts the latter definition based on records function.

Records Versus Information: A Hierarchical Order

The hierarchy of records in organizations is rarely found either in published or non-published materials. On the contrary, data and information are viewable in a hierarchical order and could be found especially from online resources. Fig. 2.1 relates the concepts of information and records with a data hierarchy (Chaffey & Wood, 2005) and shows how corporate create levels for records (Taylor, 2007). The figure is proposed from a combination of existing sources to show differences in hierarchy order, value, and meaning.

Data, information, and knowledge are interrelated. Davenport and Prusak (2000) define knowledge as the second highest order (wisdom is the highest but is not pictured here because it does not relate to this study) that is composed of data and information. Data consists of figures and facts about objects, persons and events. Analysis, processing, and classifying

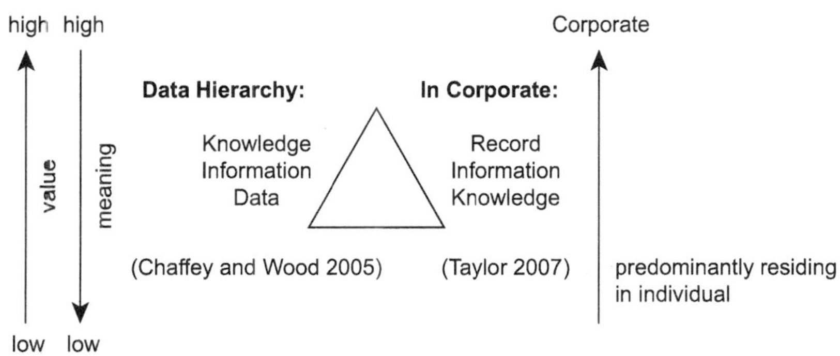

Figure 2.1 The concepts of records and information (Chaffey & Wood, 2005; Taylor, 2007).

of the data is done to produce information. Information, distilled with experience, values, insights, and intuition later becomes knowledge. The value and meaning of knowledge is greater than data and information. This concept is demonstrated in the scenario where staff members who possess greater knowledge are more valuable to the company than those who possess less.

On another note, organizations view knowledge differently when it is placed at the lowest level, compared with the highest level where it becomes a record. Knowledge resides in individuals who benefit most from it, but records are most beneficial to the organization as a whole as records may provide evidence of all business activities. Knowledge without records is not evidence and so it cannot protect the organization from legal threats.

Differences Between Electronic and Paper Records

In principle, electronic records is no different than paper records except their media for creation, storage, maintenance, management, disposal, or preservation. The media is where the commonality ends, which allows for substantial differences between the records (Rotenstreich, 2006). Although both must consist of content, context, structure, and fixity to form records, these are maintained differently in both paper or electronic.

The issues of differences are commonly discussed from the aspects of variety of record types. For example, paper records could exist in ledger, personnel files, letters, or articles; however, these types exist in electronic differently. Ledger created from spreadsheets contains formulas, charts, and serve as database. Consequently, the structure of electronic records is more complex than paper records. A description of the structure in electronic records is described as an object (document) that identifies its component parts and the nature of the relationship between those parts (Johnston, 1998). The structure allows for creating another supported sub-document, hyperlinks to other sub-sub-documents, dynamic parts that hold to web pages that can include programming languages such as JavaScript and ASP for running in the browser, and spread sheets as a result of embedded executable fields, functions, and macros. Apparently, electronic records have wider spectra than paper, because electronic system provides records from word-processed text including tables, databases, images, voices, and many other characteristics required by the users.

Electronic records are easily tampered than paper records. This could be done from the functions provided by the electronic system, which requires less effort than in paper records. This has led to redundancy and lack of control over records' trustworthiness including authenticity, reliability, and integrity. Electronic system maintains information about records; referred to as metadata, such as author's name, document creation date,, and last accessed date. The metadata is embedded in the system, and it does not appear on a hard copy of the document. This is difficult to identify changes, and hence to maintain its accuracy especially for those without IT background.

Besides disparity between electronic and paper records, there are also other issues to view from the aspects of policy, functional requirements, reference model, implementation frameworks, and risks (Bearman, 2007). The lack of policy and software tools to comply became issues recently, with required verification to control software, and requirements for evidence in human and machine enforceable terms. Severe risks also have been identified when records are no longer in control and fluid to move from one software to another (Bearman, 2006).

Despite these differences and issues found in electronic records, it does not withhold records from being created and used the records. On the contrary, electronic records have been accepted widely in the modern world to assist management to be efficient, effective, and competitive. In 2011, Obama issued an executive memorandum to enhance records information and management processes, to improve performance and promote openness and accountability by better documenting agency actions and decisions (Abraxas, 2013).

THE CONCEPT OF CLASSIFICATION FROM VARIOUS PERSPECTIVES

Classification is universal, and to classify is human. Bowker and Star (1999) postulate that classification occupies a peculiar place in studies of social order. Anthropologists, economists, historians, sociologist, information scientists, philosophers, and statisticians all have unique perspectives of classification. Anthropologists study classification as a device for better understanding cultures, while economists look at trends to project future economic growth. Historians classify to preserve heritage, and sociologists categorize individual links with social movements to diagnose certain social illness. Information scientists work every day on the practical design, delegation, and choice of classification for retrieval efficiency. Conversely, philosophers and statisticians debate classification theory but conduct few empirical studies of impact.

This section discusses the concepts of classification as found in the archival science, library science, and information science fields (Foscarini, 2009; Livelton, 1996; Orr, 2005; Xie, 2006). These fields have commonly been discussed in earlier classification research. At the end of this section is a discussion on the differences between classifications from the various perspectives.

THE ARCHIVAL SCIENCE AND RECORDS MANAGEMENT PERSPECTIVES

Archival science is a systematic body of theory that supports the practice of appraising, acquiring, authenticating, preserving, and providing access to recorded materials. It emerged from diplomatic work in the 19th century as a body of concepts and methods directed toward the study of records in terms of their documentary and functional relationships, and the ways in which they are controlled and communicated (Duranti & McNeil, 1997).

Archival science theories have contributed to the records management field, which is responsible for the systematic control of the creation, maintenance, use, and disposition of records (Pearce-Moses, 2005). There are two types of archival theories (Murdoch, 2007). The first type describes and explains archival procedures and activities, such as devising arrangement schemes, defining series, and reconstructing provenance. The second type is concerned with the content and context of records, rather than rote processes of control (Roberts, 1990).

The field of archival science plays an important role in the development of an RC system because the theory provides the basis for identifying the context, content, and structure of records, determining the authenticity and reliability of records, and preserving records from the creation to preservation stage. The classification of records operates on a principle whereby records are grouped on the basis of a function or activity (Pearce-Moses, 2005). It is based on an analysis of functions and activities in relation to organizations' mandate and business processes (Xie, 2007).

Classification is not just used as a retrieval tool. If one understands classification as a mere retrieval tool, then its role in the context of electronic records systems would be outdated or excessive, given the highly sophisticated search engines usually embedded in those systems. Therefore, to avoid misperceptions or misunderstandings of context, it is important that classification is seen as offering other value for ensuring that management is efficient, effective, and competitive (Foscarini, 2009). ICA (2008a, 2008b,

2008c) and HB 5031 (2011) assert that the classification of records enables the following:

1. work to be linked to form a continuous record of activity;
2. changes to the way business activity is described to be recorded and documented;
3. meaning to be passed on to those who may not have been directly involved in the business that was undertaken;
4. work to be distributed to appropriate people and groups;
5. management responsibility for sets of records to be distributed;
6. link to security and access permissions to be applied to records; and
7. link to disposal periods and actions to be applied to records.

Therefore, the purpose of records classification is not solely to either describe content or enable search and retrieval. Rather, records classification is most often used to support a whole suite of records management processes, including identifying records to be captured and created to support businesses and providing a structure for determining and implementing retention, security, and access decisions, as well as to place records in the context of the business activity that created them (HB 5031, 2011). Classification for recordkeeping purposes is typically used to ensure that the links between the business being performed and the resulting records are robust and maintained.

This difference is essential for records management, as it demands that information managed as classification in archival science and records management perspective plays a major role in preserving the relational links between the description of the business and the records. Its primary purpose is to link information about records, enabling the content of the record to be linked to associate events such that the "full story" can be recreated.

The contribution from archival science theory and records management practice has distinguished the function of classification from the library science and information science perspectives. This is referred to the aspects of records life cycle and trustworthiness. Records are classified based on requirements such as policy, laws, mandates, and organizations, and trustworthiness is maintained through authenticity, integrity, and reliability from creation until preservation. The value of classification is not only in daily operational activities, but strategic management and longevity of the business or organization.

THE LIBRARY SCIENCE PERSPECTIVE

Classification from the library science perspective is popularly discussed and more prevalent compared to archival science. The history of library classification is noteworthy. From the Baconian era until today, classification is observed philosophically, progressing from traditional to modern library classification. The definition of classification has evolved, but what has endured is the solid purpose of providing information retrieval.

Shupak (1974) describes classification as a mental process of ordering the universe and for the library practice; it is a mere act of storing and locating documents in a collection of materials. Philosophically, classification is a hierarchical ordering of the universe, from one concept experience to another, by revising categories while building the knowledge consistently to represent the universal order. In the 1950s, a new philosophy emerged in which library classification is considered a computer-assisted shuffling device that allows for quick, subtle, and efficient manipulations of ideas, facts, and subjects (Painter, 1974).

Library classification evolved distinctly in the United States compared to Europe and Asia. Traditional schemes were designed and used solely for browsing tools or shelf organizers, and thus tend to generally classify "one place on the shelf – one place in the scheme." On the contrary, Europeans and Asians have used classification to organize concepts specifically in indexes (classified catalogs). This difference in approach has influenced the advancement of classification around the world, while maintaining the central foundation performing efficiently to locate documents for users (Painter, 1974; Shupak, 1974).

In the early 1900s, American librarians usually referred to classification in terms of two specific library implementations: Dewey decimal classification (DDC) and the Library of Congress classification (LC). Stevenson (1974) argues that for generations librarians suffered from the habit of confusing the general idea of library classification with the possibilities and limitations of DDC and LC. This misinterpretation of library classification protected DDC and LC from further arguments. No clear distinction was made between general principles of the nature, structure, and uses of library classification and the practice of these principles in specific systems. Consequently, in the 1970s, library classification began to be perceived more traditionally, as DDC and LC usually were used for religious texts and sacred rituals identified as general classification with no subject limitations.

In the new millennium, classification has come to be perceived as a foundation of retrieval systems and the key approach to information retrieval (Szostak, 2014). Classification is a system or method for coding and organizing library materials (books, serials, audio visual materials, computer files, maps, manuscripts, teaching aid) according to subject, then allocating a call number that links to the relevant information resources (Mishra, 2010). Cataloging is also one of the important tasks of library classification (Khan, 2006). There are two parts of library classification. The first is organizing knowledge by identifying similarities between subjects, while the second is physically organizing books on shelves (Batley, 2007).

Stevenson (1974) once argued that the library classification is not a physical artifact consisting of schedules and indexes, but a process that takes place in the human mind. Nevertheless, never in the history of libraries has more been known about classification. It has been noted that classification is not a matter of picking out and conceptually grouping together certain entities of heterogeneous field into certain classes, as the process of grouping interrupts and disregards relationships between entities. He further explains that a functional organization (function-based classification) can preserve better than class organization, and it is not worth sacrificing this advantage to allow "likeness" to absorb or relocate dissimilarities in classification. However, the notion is not emphasized in the evolution of library classification, as generations of librarians learned to live with DDC and LC. This resulted in the focus of classification research resting not in librarianship, but rather in information science.

Richmond (1960) shows that the library classification in referring to LC is pragmatic and functional, remaining widely used with considerable consumer satisfaction. However, it is not logical, scientifically, nor probabilistically built. The classification system violates all the claims, principles, and laws that are considered important in classification making. It shows limited relationships in hierarchies; has little to do with language or linguistics; and sprawls arbitrarily in all directions. A classification scheme must not arbitrarily group the materials into few classes, because there may be major classes with numerous subclasses in a cross-classification mechanism (Abrera, 1974). Richmond further clarifies that a classification scheme should not be evaluated only on the basis of completeness, but rather the extent to which it advances knowledge and achieves the purpose for which it was originally created.

Theories supporting library classification were criticized for lacking substantive intellectual content (Hjørland, 2008). Jones (2005) and Szostak (2004) claim that lack of theory in library classification is because of the focus given to the application of new technology and standards, a culture of social reality and systems of activity (Bowker & Star, 1999, 2000), rather than contributing to the context or primary purpose of records. The nature of classification in library science differs from RM. Library classification keeps similar items together and dissimilar items separate in an attempt to help library users to locate the materials needed in the quickest time possible (Manoff, 2004). In contrast, in RC assigned records are based on function to maintain reliability, integrity, and authenticity from creation to preservation (Duff, 1996; Duranti, 1998, 2007; Duranti & MacNeil, 1997).

THE INFORMATION SCIENCE PERSPECTIVE

From the social respective, information science was regarded as a body of knowledge providing an understanding of the means through which society's information needs are met (Hoshovsky & Massey, 1968). Information science is an interdisciplinary field that includes such topics as behavioral science, classification, transfer, and language and linguistics (Harmon, 1971). Information science cuts across several conventional academic disciplines and the domain of information science is the universe of recorded information and knowledge. Addressing the context of recorded information, information science is the study of the gathering, organizing, storing, retrieving, and disseminating of information (Bates, 1999).

It can be deduced that information science is an interdisciplinary field concerned with the theories and practices, as well as technologies, laws, and industry dealing with knowledge transfer and the information sources; the generation, organization, processing, distribution, communication, and uses of information, as well as communications among users and their behavior as they seek to satisfy their information needs.

The scope of classification discussed in Vickery writings in early 1960s ranges from a narrow (classification per se) to broader discussion about the subject of information retrieval, reflecting the diversion between library science and information science (Broughton & Mills, 2011). Classification is associated with information science, as this field governs the flow of information and techniques to manage information for optimal storage, retrieval, and dissemination (Borko, 1968).

The idea of optimizing storage and information retrieval has amalgamated from librarianship and computer science (Saracevic, 1999). As library science focuses on classification per se, it focuses on the broader subject of information retrieval (Broughton & Mills, 2011). However, theories of classification in information science are often debated for the absence of a theoretical foundation, absence of "explicit" theories and laws, and are practice-oriented (Capurro & Hjørland, 2003; Hjørland, 2008; Webber, 2003).

COMPARISON OF CLASSIFICATIONS FROM THE ARCHIVAL, LIBRARY, AND INFORMATION SCIENCES

Comparisons of classification are normally based on the methods employed by two disciplines, archival science and library science (Foscarini, 2009; Orr, 2005; Xie, 2006). Lewinson (1939) discussed on the archives classification method later noted as "records classification" in the study. In the United States, it was considered a new and immature method compared to that used in Europe. Lewinson (1939) claimed that America had better experience with library classification and had established the basic significance of library classification, but lacked systematic groundwork in records classification. It was noted that library classification was based on three elements, namely the predetermined logical scheme of subject matter; the physical arrangement of material according to the logical scheme of subject matter; and finding of material using this scheme (Campbell, 1941). The third element has been supported by Manoff (2004) and Foscarini (2009) who stated that library classification serves as a retrieval-oriented technique. It is not, however, recommended to employ library classification methods to classify records (Leland 1915 in Schellenberg, 1956) because, "no decimal system of classification, no refined methods of library science, and no purely chronological or purely alphabetical arrangement can be successfully applied to records classification."

Table 2.1 is a summary of archival science, library science, and information science perspectives, describing the definition, theoretical philosophy, and classification approach for each. These three fields contribute important concepts to classification, and focus on different purposes, but complement each other because they are interdisciplinary. From the archival science perspective, classification is holistic and theoretically strong. Library science has seen more research undertaken about classification but it is primarily for retrieval purpose and practice. From an information science perspective, classification has evolved as the tool to optimize the process of storage, retrieval, and dissemination.

Elements of library classification are related to archival theory and the practical conditions of archival work (Greetham, 1999; Lewinson, 1939; Schwartz & Cook, 2002). For example, the physical arrangement

Table 2.1 The Summary of Classification From Various Fields

Field	Description of the Field		Notes
Information science	Definition:		The focus of classification is optimal storage, retrieval, and dissemination.
	Investigates the properties and behavior of information, the forces that govern the flow and use of information, and the techniques, both manual and mechanical, of processing information for optimal storage, retrieval and dissemination (Borko, 1968)		Relates to classification but from a technological approach.
	Theoretical philosophy	No	
	Practical philosophy	Yes	
	Approach: Not specific		
Library science	Definition:		The focus of classification is coding and organizing library material.
	Collection, organization, preservation, and dissemination of information resources and the political economy of information (Mishra, 2010).		Organizes in two ways: First, organizing knowledge by identifying similarities between subjects and, second, organizing books on shelves.
	Theoretical philosophy	No	
	Practical philosophy	Yes	Relates to classification from aspect of keeping similar items together and separate from dissimilar items, to be located in quick time.
	Approach: Subject-based, facet analysis		Retrieval-oriented.
Archival science	Definition:		The focus of classification is based on:
	Access to recorded material, appraising, acquiring, authenticating, preserving (Duranti & MacNeil, 1997).		Activity or functions, identifying context, context, and structure of records; determining the authenticity and reliability of records; and preserving records from creation to preservation.
	Theoretical philosophy	Yes	The theory provides a method to identify context, context, and structure of records, determine the authenticity and reliability of records, and preserve records from creation to preservation.
	Practical philosophy	Yes	
	Approach: Function based		

of library materials, as outlined in the second element of library classification, is governed theoretically by the principle of provenance (*respect des fond*). However, the action of assigning records to a place in a predetermined logical scheme based on subject matter, and their identification by a system of symbols representing the elements of the scheme, will not work for the classification of records. This is a determination of objective fact, not the application of an intellectual scheme. Therefore, the so-called library classification is not a classification per se, but rather an exercise in taxonomy that redefines classification used for archival purpose in a fashion, rejecting entirely any analogy with library terminology. As for records classification, it covers descriptive activities consisting of an "objective determination by appropriate techniques of legal and historical research (if necessary), of agency, of origin, of custody, and similar determination of the functional types of records represented in the collection, and boundaries, temporally, geographically, or otherwise objectively delimited" (Lewinson, 1939).

The principles of provenance (*respect des fonds*) and the principles of the sanctity of the original order (*registrazurprinzip*) have influenced the classification of records specifically and records management generally, including the writings of professionals such as Jenkinson, MacLean, Bearman, and Upward. In addition to the principles, *respect des fonds* has been equally important as the "ambient" level for recordkeeping. The concept of *respect des fonds* was developed in 1841 in France. It has been claimed as relevant to the preparation of inventories and the physical grouping of records in repositories, and acts as a classification system for recordkeeping entities. The functionality of the principal can be found in matters that deal with juridical or legal entities at a broad level but less on the internal dimensions of structure that relate to the process of creating records. Therefore, the *respect des fond* model serves as a framework that holistically defines administration bodies at a legal rather than the actual level in which records are created (Upward, 1998, pp. 110–130).

Upward (1998) also claims the two principles (*provenance* and *registrazurprinzip*) have led to a third approach to the ordering of archives, namely "...the system of classification should be based on the original organization of archives, which corresponds in its main outline, with the organization of the administration that produces it." The non-Dutch archivist claimed it has no relevance to 20th century records, and Australian experience has found it to be irrelevant. As a result, MacLean explored practical practices and approaches that extended Jenkinson's Manual and in turn led to further discussions about the archival term "classification." The term, which in North America and Australia has continually bumped against alternative usage by librarians and records managers, has appeared to fall into disrepute. The term, however, has particular meanings within archival theory and practice, which need to be considered before deciding to eliminate it.

CLASSIFICATION: MACHINE VERSUS HUMAN

Technology has become ubiquitous, dominating many aspects of library science, which has guided the librarianship toward this technology. As a result, library science has been broadened to library and information science by reconciling the fields of humanistic librarians and computer scientists. In classification, this combination has been manifested into computerized classification or automatic document classification (Moberg, 1974). Heaps (1973) views automatic document classification as a method to optimize that classify a set of test documents depending on the correlation between relevance and the mutual content of pairs of documents. Generally, documents are classified by subject matter, topic, or even with respect to phenomena. Documents are not classified according to universal schema but rather by different terminology employed by diverse disciplines (Szostak, 2008). Automatic document classification is not only able to distinguish the text, but also understands the meaning and context of words precisely, typically with the precision and recall concept (Council, 2015).

Document classification is also known as document/text categorization/routing and topic identification. Document classification may be defined as content-based assignment of one or more predefined categories (topics) to documents that can be used for document filtering and routing to topic-specific processing mechanisms such as information extraction and machine translation (Goller, Löning, Will, and Wolff, 2000). Automatic document classification is closely related to document retrieval. In document retrieval the user specifies his information need by giving a query, which is then analyzed and applied to a relatively fixed and preprocessed (indexed) document corpus. This makes it easier to find the relevant information at the right time and filter and route documents directly to users.

Automatic document classification applies machine learning or other technologies to automatically classify documents that resulted in faster, scalable, and more objective classification. There are at least three approaches:

supervised methods, unsupervised method, and rules-based method. The rule-based method is associated with higher quality performance, especially in complex scenarios (Council, 2015). With regards to automated machine learning for classifying documents, the best and most practical approach is to employ both computers and humans in the process. Software that enables humans to automate classification rules through machine learning makes things more efficient. Less effort is required to automatically classify compared to manually, because a machine performs the process and produces results independently.

Parapadakis (2013) argues that a records management is not a single requirement but has multiple requirements, including "classification," "declaration," "retention and management," and "security and auditability." Automatic classification relates to "classification" that uses linguistic, lexical, and semantic analysis, while "declaration" that decides the value of documents if worthy as records. The challenge to automating classification does not lie in "classification" but rather in "declaration." The so-called automatic declaration is not always available because it requires more than understanding the type of document and its context, which comes from the process. Automatic classification is also not new, having been implemented both as a standalone product and integrated within emails and records capture systems. However, adoption has remained slow due to compliance issues. Legal departments may be reluctant to accept that a machine can perform classification.

CONCLUSION

Classifications from other disciplines namely library and information science do not differ significantly from records management perspective. The concept of classification is the same in those disciplines, which is to select and arrange information for speedy access; precise and accurate retrieval; and smart searching. However, the application of classification differs in other disciplines because records management prioritizes that records should be managed based on its context and life cycle. The values of records can be derived from these criteria. Records management highlights on the context and life cycle of records to be included in the classification. The records created and maintained are in accordance to the records life cycle in order to protect its context for authenticity and trustworthiness. These are to be included in the records profile and metadata of the records, and referred from standards and regulations stated in organizations.

Aside from discussing concept of classification from various fields namely archival and records management, library and information science, this chapter also discusses on automatic classification and the development of classification systems from the perspective of these disciplines. The first theory from archival science remains the heart of the development of a records classification model because it provides the value to the model from the aspects of authenticity, validity, and reliability. The second and third theories from information science contribute to search and retrieval techniques, as these two functions are widely used across the discipline.

CHAPTER THREE

Function-Based Classification

INTRODUCTION

Function-based classification, also referred to as records classification in this book, emphasizes the functions of records to ensure the context of records are intact and secured over time. The terminology referring to this concept is undetermined, whereby phrases such as functional classification, function-based classification, and business classification are used (Orr, 2005; Henttonen & Kettunen, 2011). Therefore, these three terminologies are used interchangeably by the authors.

Records classification was introduced by Schellenberg by including the concept of selection in records management, emphasizing the processes involved in distinguishing official documents before permanent preservation as records (away from office of origin) and at the highest point as archives. The process is not easy because in England the terms "records" and "archives" tend to be used interchangeably, whereas in the US, the terms are distinguished based on their point of use. The primary reason why most records are preserved is to accomplish the purpose of records' creation and accumulation. Moreover, records must also be preserved for cultural reasons, and for reference and research purposes in archival institutions. Realizing the need for records to be preserved for long-term use, Schellenberg imposed a classification approach to select and keep only relevant records that have evidentiary value. The approach was based on organizations and functions, known as records- or function-based classification.

Although there were other ways to classify (documents), such as by subject, Schellenberg rejected these approaches claiming they were suitable only for reference and information files. He emphasized the importance of starting from an analysis of an agency's functions, activities, and transactions (Foscarini, 2009). On the other hand, records should be classified by function because they are the result of a function and should be used in relation to a function. It is also possible to refer to the organizational structure, if the organization is stable and its functions and administrative activities are well defined (Schellenberg, 1956; Foscarini, 2009). As a result, function-based

Records Classification: Concepts, Principles and Methods
ISBN 978-0-08-102238-2
http://dx.doi.org/10.1016/B978-0-08-102238-2.00003-2

classification is an approach that has become a point of reference for records classification not only in the United States, and the functional analysis framework (function-activity-transaction model) has become a useful reference worldwide.

There are also other factors that contributed to the records classification system such as aggregations of records, appraisal, and selection on the basis of the higher evidential and information value of records. The critical point underlying Schellenberg's model is that any predictable retention and preservation need to be taken into account. Schellenberg also made no reference to the nature of the records and theoretical considerations (such as the need for establishing and perpetuating the original context of records creation), but pragmatically concludes that records should be classified for quick retrieval whenever needed but should not be over-classified.

EVOLUTIONS OF RECORDS CLASSIFICATION

This review of classification focuses on the classification of records from the early days of registry and filing systems to modern electronic systems. The evolution of RC approaches is discussed as well as evolutions and principles of classification and reasons for choosing the latest approach to classify records based on function.

Registries, based on archival science approaches, were an early method used to administer and take responsibility for the maintenance and use of public records. The concept was introduced in Germany but developed differently in the European continent. The basic difference was its relative position in the governmental structure. In Europe, the clerical function of writing and copying letters was separated from that of providing recordkeeping services. Special offices known as "registries," gradually evolved to preserve and service current records. Registries received the divisional mail from a central clerical office. The mails were registered, indexed, and routed to the proper officials with all pertinent attachments. The returned mails were then classified in accordance with an established scheme of classification following the four processes (register→index→classification→inventories) as follows:

1. registers consisting of ledgers or card files containing entries for the individual documents in consecutive numerical order;
2. indexes to persons and subjects;
3. classification schemes indicating the subject headings under which the records were physically arranged; and

4. inventories, showing the actual files kept in accordance with the classification scheme.

Posner's observations on this early system showed the tendency to super-rationalize and over-refine sub-partitions of records. It was claimed to be complicated and was gradually replaced by more simple and logical classification schemes. Practical-inductive principles of classification evolved in the 16th and 17th centuries, and were followed by rational-deductive principles in the 18th century.

On the contrary, there was little occasion to develop theories about the classification of inactive records in England, because the records were relegated without a selection process to storage—The Golden Rule of Archiving. The lack of theoretical development also stemmed from how records and archives were perceived. In England, records and archives were similar things; therefore all records, either from active or inactive phases, are acquired in the storage.

Germany, renowned for its administrative efficiency, developed a revolutionary new method to organize records made and received by the government in the 17th and 18th centuries. All records were primarily related to the same subject, and secondarily to a given business transaction, activity, or procedure, independent of their status of transmission (i.e., the degree of perfection, e.g., draft, original, or copy), form, or value. The records would be incrementally put together in separate physical and logical units, called *dossiers* or files, which would then in turn be combined organically according to various homogeneous criteria such as names of persons or corporate bodies, geographic units, subject-matters, or dates, a system known as *Registratursysteme* (Foscarini, 2009). This was the first example of a systematic method of classifying records according to a comprehensive, subject- and function-based *Aktenplan* (i.e., file plan). The effectiveness of such a "mixed model" of classification was related to it being a natural way of carrying out administrative work that was itself very rational, linear, and rigorous. Fig. 3.1 represents the timeline beginning from 17th century to 20th century of early classification system.

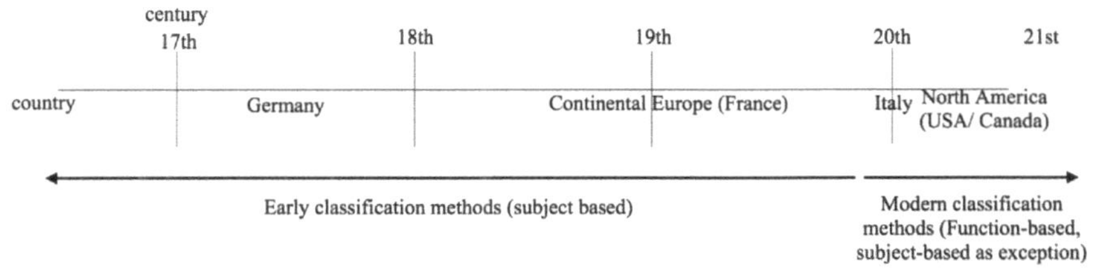

Figure 3.1 Early and modern classification system timeline.

The German system claimed to be systematic and advanced; however, a *posteriori*, ex-post is a flaw in the system (Foscarini, 2009). As a consequence, explicit links among the interrelated records of a business transaction were established when the activity of the records referred to was concluded and the relevant file was transferred to the central registry, rather than concurrently with the creation of the records and the development of the activity generating them. Hence, critics suggested that the "original order" of the records was artificially created for the sake of administrative control.

At the beginning of the 19th century, the German system spread throughout most of continental Europe as a consequence of the conquests made by Napoleon, whose administration adopted and improved the system by combining classification and registration capabilities into a single tool. The systematic identification and pre-organization of all incoming and outgoing correspondence was subsequently extended to cover internal records as well. With these adjustments, classification became the heart of the Napoleonic administrative system.

The Italian system, credited by the legal system, developed a method for the classification and registration of records in the mid-20th century. Writings from Raffaele De Felice broadly discussed the topic of records classification from both a conceptual and a methodological view. De Felice viewed classification as systematic, designing the system with an organic, logical, and coherent method. He claimed that classification was systematic "by competence," using activity, and office interchangeably (Foscarini, 2009). Although De Felice did not define "competence" in his writings, it was defined as the authority and capacity for carrying out activities within one function conducted by given office or individual. The use of competence in his writings reflected the function-activity-transaction notion, later proposed by Schellenberg in 1950s.

In the United States, records classification has been accredited when facing the problem of storage due to massive documents created. It is noted clearly by Schellenberg that "Modern public records are very voluminous" and it would not stop at certain level because as human population grows and develops new technology, the records produced will increase in mass exponentially. The need to reduce documents quantity is crucial and only those with archival value should be preserved. At that time, the concern was how to know and keep the records that have value, while the assessment of records' value became secondary. Hence, Schellenberg set up a standard of determining the records' evidential and informational value that aimed at appraising a document's evidential and information value which include things like the uniqueness of the document, its function, and form, and how it relates to the overall scheme of an organization. The theory that Schellenberg developed in response to his environment thus stressed the need to reduce bulk by selecting from among the masses of documentation that which was permanently valuable, and to make this selection intelligently available to researcher (Stapleton, 1983–84).

Recent study by Foscarini (2009) has suggested a classification system structured "by competence" will be "function-based" to the extent that the organizational structure corresponds to the hierarchy of functions and activities attributed to any given entity. But, classification does not affect administrative change because its flexibility is constrained by the organizational setting. This organizational setting informs its structure not the administrative change. Therefore, "competence" is one of the variables (competence, cognitive act, and archival bond) in the classification system offered by De Felice. The cognitive act of classification is to guarantee the correct formation of the series through the rational categorization of the competences of the office and the archival bond, to determine the internal structure of archival fonds, and therefore in his view, classification becomes "the only means to accomplish the formation of archives."

THE RATIONALES OF CLASSIFYING INFORMATION BY FUNCTION

Although function-based classification is claimed to be more relevant than subject-based classification, it is still common practice to classify records based on subject content (LAC, 2006a, 2006b). The shift in this practice took place from the 1980s when archivists started to insist on functional analysis and micro appraisal. The current trend for classification is aligned with function-based concepts, based on rigorous analysis of business functions and activities. Function-based classification is a logical arrangement of all records documenting or evidencing the activities of an institution based upon an analysis of the institution's business functions, sub-functions, and activities. Function-based analysis focuses on the accountability agenda of an institution and, in so doing, situates records within their operational or administrative context in an order that reflects the sequence in which those activities and/or events take place. Library and Archives Canada (LAC) believes that function-based classification systems will prove to be more effective and enduring because they are based on an analysis of the actual business activities and processes of the institution rather than the subject content of documents, organizational structures that frequently change, or other characteristics upon which records classification systems were traditionally constructed (Foscarini, 2009).

Subject-based classification is not suitable for archival material because that material is concerned about the trustworthiness of material and its archival *fonds*. Subject-based classification tends to dissolve the *fonds* of archival materials, because they (the materials) are referred to by their contents and subjects. For example, salary records that were created in the finance department, but kept in a personal file. According to *fonds*, all documents that originate from the same source must be compiled together without breaking the connection of its link. Accordingly, salary records should be kept in the finance department because that was the place where they were first created. Subject-based classification does not consider this principle, and is only concerned with the subject or content within the records.

Methodologies to design a function-based classification system are few. One of them is the business activity structure classification system (BASCS). The BASCS rests on the assumption that the sequence of procedural steps that are described in, and often prescribed by, legislation or other regulatory instruments potentially make up the structure of a given type of activity. The term "activity structure" in the acronym BASCS, was meant by its developers to describe the decomposition of functions and activities according to both a hierarchical and a sequential order (not an alphabetical one), down to the elementary units that correspond to the steps, or transactions, generating the actual files. According to this approach, the latter would thus reflect the natural (either prescribed or logical) development of each activity carried out by an agency.

Even so, there are still limitations in strict interpretations of the function-based approach of classification as described by Sabourin (2001), which could result in an abstract and self-referential system, a classification that might reflect the functions of the organization, yet would be totally unable to capture the actual ways of carrying out work in a real office.

A second shortcoming refers to the fact that not every single activity behaves as a structured, repetitive process. There are areas of human endeavor (e.g., academic research, teaching, or artistic performance) that, on the contrary, have the characteristic of being creative and unpredictable, so that the relevant activities do by no means follow any preestablished, linear, or cyclical sequence of steps. Such a "freedom of action," following the "soft systems thinking approach," is related to the nature of human beings who can always "decide to act otherwise" and who may as well enter in any work procedures, even the most bureaucratic ones. This implies that a fully function-based approach of classification is destined to fail due to its own abstractness and "perfection."

A last, record-related consideration inspired by the Canadian model is that, in a real work environment, not every step that makes up a process is bound to generate a distinct transaction file, as assumed by BASCS. Some offices may find it more convenient for the purposes of their business, for instance, to keep all of the records originated by an entire process, or even an entire function, together in one single file. In such a case, the higher activity level, not the transaction level, should be tagged as the entry point for file creation. Where the main driver for classification design is the workflow, rather than being the records flow or the user needs, the lower levels of the scheme tend to become too detailed and as such, they may cause excessive fragmentation of files. As a consequence, users may find the classification complicated to apply and record keepers may have difficulty in keeping it up to date.

THE ELEMENTS OF CLASSIFICATION

Classification is made up of three elements. These are physical action, scheme, and logic (Schellenberg, 1956; Savic, 1995). Physical action is regarded as the user interface, use, and achieved result; scheme is regarded as the knowledge base; and logic is the inference engine. Therefore, classification does not stand alone but requires a user interface, knowledge, and engine to work. This places records classification in the element of scheme, a core point, which must be considered prior to developing a system. In addition, classification needs a solid foundation and technique so as to enable the implementation of the system to work well. The arbitrary use of this concept may jeopardize the organization in the long run while impairing system efficiency. This is evident in the actual practice where many electronic document management system have to be reviewed and revised (Xie, 2008).

In records management, purposes of classification include protecting the confidentiality of records, managing retention schedules, assisting with the retrieval of records in context, and managing workflows (Sabourin, 2001; Yusof & Chell, 2005; Foscarini, 2009; Yusof, 2009; HB 5031, 2011). Classification has been viewed as a form of roadmap that provides rules and definitions, from the creation of records to their disposal (Xie, 2006). This is to ensure that records can be identified and located, used and understood across time (HB 5031, 2011), with stable and fixed content, and correspond to a template made up of four sections: documentary form, annotations, context, and medium (InterPARES1, 2002). Records classification must also include document relationships, in order to assure authenticity and reliability.

CLASSIFICATION DESIGN

The design of records classification should be consistent with or comply with legislation, regulations, international standards, and the characteristics of documents, as well as an organization's business needs (Chosky, 2006). For records classification to be successfully implemented, the structure of an organization must be understood. The life cycle and the value of the documents also need to be determined since not all documents are records. Thus, it is important to distinguish classification within the ambit of a retention schedule.

The principles of records classification, when applied either manually or electronically, could have a significant impact on the management of records. On their own, computer systems are not likely to be successful in managing records, because they require a systematic, efficient, and effective document retrieval process, the management of records retention, the assigning of access privileges, the protection of records confidentiality, the retrieval of records in context, and the management of workflows (Foscarini, 2009; Yusof & Chell, 2005; Yusof, 2009). Furthermore, records management may help Malaysia in realizing Vision 2020, but it has not been given a high priority (Yusof & Chell, 2005). Therefore, the evolution of IT applications no longer focuses on technical aspects only but also nontechnical aspects such as arranging documents based on records classification; identifying documents and records; valuing records; appraising records; and labeling records for retention purposes. This is the impact of records evolution and better understanding on the importance of records for business and nation (Cook, 1992).

It is common in document and information retrieval to state that classification should be involved at documenting of the description, storage, and retrieval process. Classification could be implemented to simplify searching or to provide a set of document descriptors to optimize requests for document matching. More sophisticated approaches also involve requests for classification. In contrast, manual classification works differently because it is a manual process and can lead to human error. For example, it does not examine the principles on which it is based in a critical way, formulate them properly, or apply them consistently (Jones, 1970, 2005). The setbacks of manual classification are controllable when the principles of records classification are introduced in systematic manner, function-based, subject-based, structure-based, or even type-based methods (Schellenberg, 1956; Foscarini, 2009). These principles have been introduced to accommodate the needs and requirements of organizations particularly government agencies. Most of the research conducted in this area depicts a good response toward the principles proposed and has evolved positively from subject-based to function-based (Schellenberg, 1956; LAC, 2006a, 2006b).

IS RECORDS CLASSIFICATION PERVASIVE?

It is commonly reported that many organizations globally did not embrace records classification in particular and records management in general. Therefore, the authors seek to find out whether records classification is ever pervasive by analyzing works or research by previous scholars in this area. The rapidness in such studies could indicate the seriousness of classifying records across the globe.

Classification in archival theory has developed and changed drastically for over the past 120 years. Records management field was introduced in mid-20th century by adapting archival, laws, and management theories. Classification is the core function for managing records, as records management is the field of managing records systematically by assisting in decision making and maintenance based on life cycles of records. The urge from past studies showed that classification is the core element in record management. Without classification, records management cannot be executed in accordance with the international standards. The classification becomes the important function because records have life cycle of use, from creation until preservation. Classification can help to manage records effectively and efficiently guiding from life cycle (current, semi-current, and no-active). Keeping no-active records in a system is a waste for storage and could affect to service performance. On the other hand, records have its value: vital, important, useful, and non-important. These categories help to categorize records for future reference.

Classification helps to provide trustworthy and authentic records if required by laws. Electronic system acts as a tool to process documents and to manipulate date according to users' needs. The documents are processed and manipulated to provide effective and efficient service in the form of speed, system reliability, and precise results. These criteria are catered in the Syariah Court Case Management System. The Syariah Court Case Management System considered the criteria only from IT perspectives. Documents, which later become records, are stored in the system, and without any guidance from records management their perspective is insecure. The records are at risk either from loss or being tampered by unauthorized persons. The implication is nothing if the document category is not-important, but for vital or important records, the affect is severe and can collapse the organization, e.g., as happened to multinational companies like Enron, Arthur Anderson, and Blitz USA Inc. In Malaysia, the loss of Pulau Batu Puteh to Singapore is one of the examples that could happen again, if vital records (electronic or paper) are not managed well. Before any disastrous case occurs again, the needs of classification is crucial to be included in the system for both paper and electronic media.

Records classification has gained its attention after the Pittsburgh project in 1997 although Schellenberg has discussed on the issue since early 1940s. The summary of previous works is tabulated in Table 3.1. The attention was not specifically given to the classification aspect, but to the entire life-cycle process including records-making until the disposal.

Despite the crucial role played by records management, many organizations pay little attention to the initiative (Wallace, 2004; Mnjama, 2004; Ngulube, 2004; Chinyemba & Ngulube, 2005). The trends in case studies in South African public agencies revealed that 98% respondents are aware of having a formal records management initiative but only 30.77% and 11.54% scored good and excellent ratings, respectively. Whereas, 57.7% rated average, poor, and very poor. The ratings indicated that records management was not an objective in the case study strategic plan (Ngoepe, 2008). This scenario explained why classification, as a function in the entire records life cycle, is under researched.

This section review previous works related to the classification of records. Stapleton (1983–84) discussed the arrangement and appraisal based on Schellenberg's views, while Carter (1998) focused on the arrangement of records solely. Martin (1987) has sparked the discussion about classification in 1987 but evolved around the archival point of view. Martin did not discuss classification explicitly but rather referring to indexing procedure as a prerequisite in overcoming unprecedented flood of documents. Indexing involves both controlled and uncontrolled vocabulary whereby classification scheme plays its role.

Table 3.1 Summary on previous works on records classification

Author	Scope	Method	Research Subject Scope					Findings
			Indexing	Classification (paper)	Classification (Electronic)	Appraisal	Arrangement	
Stapleton (1983–84)	Schellenberg's ideas on appraisal, description, and arrangement	Document content analysis	x	x	x	√	√	Schellenberg skilfully blended the archival theory and practice.
Martin (1987)	Archival indexing	Document content analysis	√	x	x	x	x	Indexing procedure as a prerequisite in overcoming unprecedented flood of documents.
The Pittsburgh project (1997)	Functional requirements and metadata	Warrant	x	√	√	x	x	Model for developing functional requirements and metadata specifications based on warrant.
Carter (1998)	Methodology of arrangement	Case study	x	x	x	x	√	Difficulties in arrangement practice and methods of arrangement using basic attributes of fonds and series
InterPARES1 (2002) and InterPARES2 (2008)	Framework for preservation developments	Diplomatics Case study	x	√	√	√	x	Requirements for authentic electronic textual records in database system

Continued

Table 3.1 Summary on previous works on records classification—cont'd

			Research Subject Scope					
Author	**Scope**	**Method**	**Indexing**	**Classification (paper)**	**Classification (Electronic)**	**Appraisal**	**Arrangement**	**Findings**
MoReqs (2001–2011)	Functional requirements	Case study	x	√	√	x	x	Common set of requirements for whole records life cycle.
NOARK 4 (2002) and NOARK 5 (2009)	Recordkeeping requirement	Case study	x	√	√	√	x	Basic recordkeeping requirements for entire life cycle of records
Wallace (2004), Mnjama (2004), Ngulube (2004, 2006) and Chinyemba & Ngulube (2005)	South African public agencies	Case study	x	x	x	x	x	Awareness on RM initiative: 30.77%. Low awareness has led to less priority to do research in records classification.
Orr (2005)	Functional approach is a practicable method of classifying records	Delphi technique and questionnaire survey	x	√	x	x	x	• Function-based classification is a valuable way of classifying records. • Exists no common model saying how functional schemes should look like. • Records managers find the model is difficult to understand and to apply.
DIRKS (2006a, 2006b, 2006c, 2006d)	Recordkeeping	Case study	x	√	√	√	x	Strategies and methodology for documenting government business.

Xie (2006)	Evaluation of the EDRMS implementation within Canadian municipality	Case study and questionnaire/interview	x	x	√	x	x	Convey significance contributions to the development of EDRMS in the aspect of classification in Canada.
e-SPARK (2008)	Consist of policy, specifications, and requirements for managing electronic records	Case study	x	x	√	√	x	There is neither a specific rule to determine the success of the system, nor guided requirements to be followed, but only generic guidelines which can be used as a reference if required.
Ngoepe (2008)	Manual records classification and training	Case study	x	√	x	x	x	The records classification system was done according to dates, directorates or subjects.
Foscarini (2009)	Function-based classification systems in central banks in Canada	Case study and questionnaire/interview	x	√	√	x	x	Methods for classification in banking sector. The perception of electronic and manual classifications.
Johare and Hussin (2010)	Functional requirements	Document content analysis	x	√	√	√	x	Classification in functional requirements and standards received less priority.
Krahn (2012)	Origins and evolutions of functional requirement	Document content analysis	x	x	√	x	x	Functional requirements to provide specifications for the electronic recordkeeping systems in order to produce trustworthy records.

In the 2000s, works in classification has extended from indexing into function-based. Projects such as Pittsburgh project (1997), InterPARES (2000–to till date), MoReqs (2001–2011), NOARK 4 (2002), NOARK 5 (2009), DIRKS (2006a, 2006b, 2006c, 2006d), and e-SPARK (2008) are also paying attention to classification. Classification is becoming prevalent and gaining its significance as more research is carried out, such as Orr (2005), Xie (2006), Ngoepe (2008), Foscarini (2009), Johare and Hussin (2010), and Krahn (2012). However, research focuses on various aspects. For example, Ngoepe focused on records management, while Johare and Hussin focused on the functional requirements. However, both were referring to similar subject matter, the classification.

Orr's study bears interesting consequences with reference to function-based classification development. The main objective of Orr's study was to understand whether the functional approach is indeed "a practicable method of classifying records." The method employed in this study was Delphi technique, which allowed to obtain the views of experts, and a questionnaire survey of records management practitioners in Australia, Canada, and the UK. The main finding of Orr's research is that, although both academic experts and practitioners seem to agree that function-based classification is a valuable way of classifying records, there exists no common model saying how functional schemes should look like, and records managers find the model difficult to understand and apply. Therefore, findings from Orr's study contribute to the usability issues around functional approach. The academic experts and practitioners could not achieve the understanding of how to develop a model which causes no difficulty for the practitioner to apply.

Xie (2006) reported on a program evaluation of the implementation and operation of an electronic document/record management system (EDRMS) program within Canadian municipality. Classifying documents is important for records management purposes. However, supplying classification codes for documents in accordance with the city's universal file plan is not easy. Among 50 respondents, 10 were uncertain about experience with classifying documents, which indicated that classifying may be sometimes easy and other times difficult; 17 respondents agreed that classifying is difficult; and 27 respondents further identified classification difficulties through factors such as years of experience and computer skills. However, results showed no correlation between years of experience and classifying documents. Likewise, the skilled and efficient computer users also do not convey a significant correlation with classifying documents. The computer skills are referred to general understanding of the Windows operating systems and common applications of personal computers. The study revealed there are other factors affecting the classification of documents, such as adequacy of training, design of file plan, and technical hindrance.

The design of file plan in the case study was a mix of function- and subject-based. The highest level is function-based and the primary, secondary, and tertiary levels are subject-based. The difficulty occurred when there are too many levels and choices in the file classification system, and time spent to find the right document is long. Moreover, classifying information is subjective and leads to different file naming for the same documents. Consequently, the documents are classified in scattered locations. The classification system also does not accommodate user's needs.

On another note, technical hindrance fetched 59% responses, from the aspect of lack of explanatory information for each category at each level. The index and search function are proposed to accommodate users' different information seeking habits and the result of search is less effective. Therefore, a thesaurus is needed to facilitate the use of controlled vocabulary.

The suggestions to overcome difficulties in classifying documents include incorporating users' needs into the design of a classification system. This is to differentiate general inputs, which do not address individual user's classification needs. However, the analysis of individual user's needs must be done separately from user profiles in EDRMS. The purpose is to gather information for control and management. The incorporation of user needs is at the transaction level of the classification system and based on an analysis of user's job tasks.

Xie's findings significantly contribute to the development of EDRMS in the aspect of classification in Canada. On the contrary, in South Africa, records are still classified manually. The findings revealed that the case study has a records classification system for paper records provided by National Archives and that 63.4% indicated to receive the training. However, the training was not sufficient because it was done only once for 1–4 h (Ngoepe, 2008). The records classification system was done according to dates, directorates, or subjects. There are no further explanations on classification aspect as the study is focused on the records management initiative at public sectors. It is agreed that records government is the foundation for government needs toward its citizens, such as to provide efficient services, be accountable, and protect citizens' rights (Fust & Graf, 2002). These could be achieved by establishing systematic controls at every stage of records life cycle in accordance with established principles and recognized records management models (Chinyemba & Ngulube, 2005). Records play crucial roles in protecting business longevity, legal attacks, and citizens' rights such as ownership of land, pensions of employees, memorandum of agreements, or business deals documentations. Hence, records management initiative has to ensure that records are retrievable, authentic, reliable, and trustworthy to act as evidence. The failure to provide records as evidence leads to loss of land, money, and business.

Another case study was conducted on the function-based classification systems in central banks in Canada (Foscarini, 2009). Statistically, the function-based classification scored the highest result, i.e., 43%, thus confirming the popularity of the method used. About 79% respondents agreed that records were managed electronically and 72% of the systems have incorporated the classification function. The classification system consisted of mixed methods, from subject-based, records schedules, organization-based, function-based, and mixed-based. The existing EDMS has folder structure and basic metadata, the mechanism to manage the life cycle of electronic records but a classification system mapped against a retention schedule was completely missing. Because the organizations were still in transition phase, and the market for EDMS/EDRMS were not mature yet, therefore nobody managed electronic records well.

The finding also revealed that "first IT revolution" in records-related matters was a result of not careful planned process. This is due to the users' urge to modernize tools, which the records professionals would accept with the unsatisfactory compromise offered by the available technology for quickest, easiest, and cheapest solution to a problem that still needed to be precisely identified. Information specialist component such as archivist, records managers, and librarians were excluded from the IT team. IT team focused on search and retrieval, and managed to dismiss any archival demands such as function-based classification to a subordinate place in the system. As a result, the classification data was nothing more than a keyword that would not provide the records in the system with any structure. The classification system in the EDMS has no function at all, but from IT perspective, the way records are structured in the system does not really matter, as long as the user can locate the records. However, for information specialist, the important criteria is to know why the information is stored in a certain way rather than where the information is stored.

The study claimed that classification for electronic records is yet to be carried out. Both the information and IT specialists have viewed classification differently. The former perceived classification as a framework for managing records throughout the life cycle that, based on the value of the information and its sensitivity, gives a structure that shows how things progress, and is able to support retention. Classification that supports only retrieval is not a classification, because even indexing is capable of doing that. On the contrary, the IT specialist perceived classification as retrieval tool. The differing perceptions are evident in the current EDMS classification.

Classification in functional requirements and standards received less than 10% coverage. Johare and Hussin (2010) reported that classification is mentioned 6.28%, 9.6%, 6.94%, 4.41%, 1.63%, 0%, and 4.94%, respectively in each guideline reviewed. The analyses were gained from seven separate guidelines (GL) covering from reference to classification. These guidelines were referred to as GL1, GL2, GL3, GL4, GL5, GL6 and GL7; in detail as GL1: Principles and Functional Requirements for Records in Electronic Office Environment: Guidelines and Functional Requirements for Electronic Records Management System (International Council on Archive ICA, 2008a, 2008b, 2008c); GL2: Model Requirements for Electronic Records Management (Moreq2) (MoReq2, 2008); GL3: Electronic Records Management Software Applications Design Criteria Standard, DoD5015-02-STD (US Department of Defense, 2007); GL4: Functional Specification for Electronic Records Management System Software (National Archives of Australia, 2008), GL5: Requirements for Electronic Records Management System Functional requirement (United Kingdom Public Record Office, 2002, pp. 1–4); GL6: Requirements for Assessing and Maintaining the Authenticity of Electronic Records (InterPARES1, 2002); and GL7: Electronic Records Management System: System Specification for Public Office (National Archives of Malaysia, 2008).

The details of the requirements and the percentage of coverage are depicted in Table 3.2. The results showed classification, in comparison with

Table 3.2 Guidelines (GL) vs classification

GL Element	GL1 (%)	GL2 (%)	GL3 (%)	GL4 (%)	GL5 (%)	GL6 (%)	GL7 (%)
Classification	6.28	9.6	6.94	4.41	1.63	0	4.94
Retention and disposal	9.14	6.06	18.91	8.09	18.86	4.43	7.02
Search, retrieve, render	5.9	4	0.86	4.85	5.01	1.26	5

retention and disposal, has gained less attention based on the research by Johare and Hussin (2010). The other elements related to classification such as search, retrieve, and render (outcomes from classification process) also received less attention than retention and disposal.

Classification benefits the whole life cycle of records, acts as one of the records management core elements, and contributes to the efficiency, effectiveness, and competitiveness of the organization. However, classification failed to gain better coverage than other processes such as retention and disposal. Without classification, retention and disposal processes fail to be conducted properly and compliantly (Morelli, 2005).

Another research was conducted for the functional requirements of electronic recordkeeping systems by Krahn (2012). There are many national and functional requirements to provide specifications for the electronic recordkeeping systems in order to produce trustworthy records. The study focused on four projects: DoD 5015.2-STD, InterPARES, functional requirements from Norway, the UK, the European Commission, Australia, the International Council of Archives (ICA) and the International Organization for Standardization (ISO), and software specifications and procedural guidance.

The DoD 5015.2-STD is a design specification for records management application. It specifies the capabilities to ensure reliability and authenticity in records, but for the creation, classification, maintenance, and disposition only of the active records. The metadata provides for long-term preservation of records including the appraisal, selection, description, and preservation, and references of archival records are incidental to the primary function of the management of current or active records. The DoD 5015.2-STD has become a de facto standard for electronic records management software applications. The standard is understood by the US Department of Defense, because it supported a testing regime but is not suitable and practical for smaller organization, which lacks the formalized records management policy and organizational structure. The standard is also irrelevant for personal, private digital records created by individuals, families, and small organizations. The standards do not prescribe how the requirements will be fulfilled, do not provide a guide to configure application, and do not provide specifications for long-term preservation of trustworthy electronic records.

The benchmark and baseline requirements produced by the InterPARES project are not system specifications, which can be tested and used to design software applications and recordkeeping systems, but rather offer procedural guidance for the creation, use, and preservation of electronic records. The guidance caters to creators and preserver that represent both individual and organizational entities to create, maintain, and preserve reliable and trustworthy electronic records over time. The presentation of guidance is articulated basic elements, which contribute to reliability and authenticity, along with recommendations for creators and preservers to ensure that the records possess these characteristics.

Various countries and international archives council, such as Norway, the UK, the European Commission, Australia, ICA, and ISO shared basic concepts, strategies, terminology, and accompanying tools in their proposed functional requirements. Model requirements for the management of electronic records (MoReq) is adopted by European countries, and the ICA/ISO standards were developed to align rather than compete with it. MoReq2, the revised and upgraded version of MoReq, first issued by the European Commission in 2001, did not explicitly mention classification but stated that "the classification scheme lies at the heart of any electronic records management system."

The first requirement that any classification scheme must fulfill, in the digital as well as in the paper world, is "to reflect in its internal organisation the hierarchical structure of business functions." MoReq2 does not go further in the elucidation of this statement, nor does it dwell upon methods of functional analysis. It is also not within its scope to explain the meaning of a business function. One of its main concerns is ensuring that the internal integrity of an ERMS is guaranteed and maintained all the times. To this end, a number of control mechanisms and user access restrictions are identified and described in detail. By technically limiting the authority to make changes to any critical metadata—including classification code—to the system administrator, MoReq2 requirements ensure that content, structure, and contextual relationships of records and files are kept unaltered, thus providing a framework to establish the authenticity of an electronic records management system's contents.

The latest version of MoReq is Moreq2010. It has potential implications for standards because it addresses the management of electronic records in any business system, not only in traditional ERMS/EDRMS applications, and extends the importance and need for recordkeeping requirements to be made available in all business systems (Warland & Lappin, 2011). Therefore, it establishes "a definition of a common set of core services that [can be] shared by many different types of records systems," which was a limitation in Moreq2. Fig. 3.2 depicts the definition in Moreq2010. The classification based on functions, activities and transactions is used to link the record with the business process.

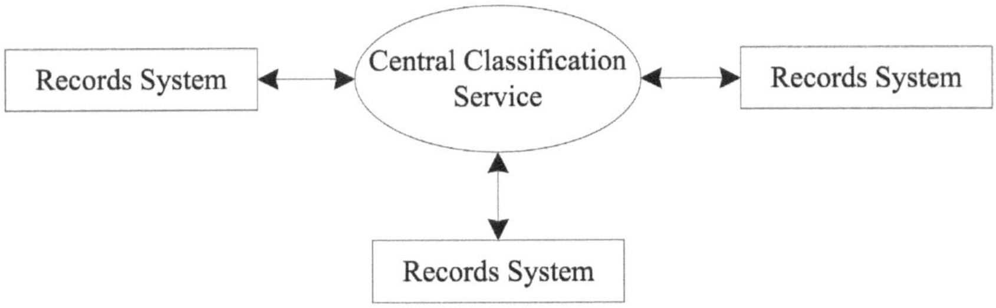

Figure 3.2 Moreq2010 (2011).

In the UK, The National Archives of the United Kingdom (TNA, formerly the Public Record Office) has promoted the use of function-based classification for the management of electronic records since the end of the 1990s (TNA, 1999). The main advantage associated with a functional approach would be that of "making the relevant records easier to identify and relocate during times of administrative change" (Todd, 2003). More recently, however, TNA has slightly modified its view and recommends a "hybrid approach," where only the higher levels of the classification are function-based, while subclasses are subject-based. A hybrid approach is considered "more achievable" than a "purist functional" one, which anyway can never be applied as such because "a degree of compromise" is always necessarily be brought in. The main difficulties refer to the fact that, first, "users do not understand and dislike (function-based classification schemes) because they are hard to use"; and second, "a strict functional approach will not support case files well" (TNA, 1999).

Foscarini (2009) asserts that the absence of empirical studies about user acceptance was the reason for the functional approach limitation. In contrast, TNA assumed limitations in the functional approach have affected the user acceptance. The claims from TNA regarding the unsuitability of functional approach to classify case files disputed with another finding from Foscarini. The finding suggests case files contents are often cross-functional and refer to individuals or other subjects, and do not cause problems particularly in an electronic environment. Shepherd and Yeo (2003) have supported the finding by giving examples on how to classify "instances of a process" by function.

In Malaysia, the body responsible for providing advice on the management of records in government agencies is the National Archives of Malaysia, which has adopted the International Council of Archives' Principles and Functional requirements for Records in Electronic Environments as a reference. Although the National Archives of Malaysia provides advice to government agencies that seek advice, it is not responsible for developing classification system. This is because classification system need to be developed based on the specific functions requirements related to the agency. There is neither a specific rule to determine the success of the system, nor guided requirements to be followed, but only generic guidelines which can be used as a reference, if required.

Therefore, this study seeks to propose a new holistic function-based classification model to be adopted by public agencies in Malaysia, taking into consideration all generic requirements and existing methods. From the analysis of existing models it was identified that 3 out of 20 are functional models for classifying records, which employed functional modeling technique. However, these models are with limitations. The UK BCS and HB 5031 models address entire aspects of RM and focus on the issue of preservation, while the DoD RMFI model focuses on the creation of records without accentuating a classification process thoroughly.

CONCLUSION

The gaps identified by the three disciplines namely archival science, library science and information science have broached the notion of integrating several theories for the development of a holistic model for records classification. Current works on records classification do not embrace all the three disciplines. For example Orr (2005) and Livelton (1996) only consider archival science while Xie (2006) work on both archival and information science. Only Foscarini (2009) considered all three disciplines focusing on the function-based classification system in Canada. It is, therefore, that the authors would like to propose the integration of relevant theories to support the development of records classification system for government agencies.

CHAPTER FOUR

Records Management Models

INTRODUCTION

This book attempts to propose a new records classification model since the existing models are generic, represented in lengthy textual form, and presented together either with functional requirements or guidelines. However, records classification model is scarce. This chapter reviews the broader and more general records management models with the aim to forecast the inadequacy of classification model which warrants a new model be proposed. The new proposed model is represented in function modeling of records classification that includes all elements and activities for classifying records. The function modeling is believed to enable the communication between IT and records management people. The existing classification models are either functional or conceptual. All of the models reviewed in this chapter relate in one way or another to records management and include a variety of similar elements, including functional requirements, standards and guidelines, handbooks, and design recommendations.

THE EXISTING RECORDS MANAGEMENT MODELS

A model is defined as a three dimensional representation of a person or thing of a proposed structure, a smaller than the real object, or a simple description of the object (Cambridge Dictionary; Hestenes, 1996). Model may have various types, structures, and domains. A model used to represent a structured function, within the subject area or system is known as function/functional model (IDEF, 1993). Structure of the model is viewed from systemic perspective, which consists of internal parts of the system (composition), external agents linked to the system (environment), and external and internal causal links (connection) (Hestenes, 1996).

Models generally take the form of inputs, processes, and outputs or expected results (Carleton College, 2009) in a simplified representation of a limited part of reality with related elements (Fishery Glossary, 1996; Pearce-Moses, 2005). Models can also exist in many forms, including scientific,

Records Classification: Concepts, Principles and Methods
ISBN 978-0-08-102238-2
http://dx.doi.org/10.1016/B978-0-08-102238-2.00004-4

mathematical and statistical, conceptual, functional, or as visualizations. They are typically represented in graphical or textual form, and often present a simplified version of a concept, phenomenon, relationship, structure, system, or aspect of the real world (Business Dictionary, n.d; Pearce-Moses, 2005; Carleton College, 2009). Models can help to facilitate an understanding of something by displaying only the necessary components, to help in decision making by simulating "what if" scenarios, and to explain, control, and predict the events on the basis of past observations. Real world scenarios are complicated and may consist of numerous functions. They may have many complex interconnections between one element and another. This complexity can be difficult to represent. Therefore, models usually depict only related functions that are of primary importance, with elements of the actual situation mapped into the model itself.

Functional models are structured representations of functions in a modeled system or subject area (FIPS, 1993). Process and activity models are similar, providing graphical representations of an organization's functions within a defined scope (DoD, 2003). On the other hand, conceptual models, such as qualitative models, help to highlight important connections in real world systems and processes, and are usually used as a foundation for the development of more complex systems (Carleton College, 2009). A functional modeling relates to the modeling of objects or relations, which construct algorithms of process for achieving the objectives, from a functional representation of the modeled entity without need to represent its real construction (Gadomski, 2006; Ford, 2009).

Records classification models are usually represented as a conceptual model type, one that may form the basis for generic and high-level models. These type of models contain a lengthy textual explanation that include an introduction, best practices and guiding principles, a description of implementation and technical issues, and a glossary. By contrast, functional models used for function-based classification depict all processes involved, from inputs, processes, and outputs, with both high-level and low-level views with extensive structured explanations. This is to ensure that the process flows are depicted smoothly and explanations are clear.

Classification models should include all elements related to classification including concepts and precepts of classification development, a plan or schema for implementation, and the way it will be implemented or deployed (Upward, 1998, pp. 110–130). Another important element is to clearly describe the way functions will be developed to establish better communications between records managers and IT experts. The processes involved would likely be depicted as a graphical model. This would benefit organizations in terms of reducing gaps in the use of terminology, concepts, and applications between records management and IT, and promote good partnerships which, eventually, could reduce the failure of records management system implementations.

The review of records management models in this chapter provides critical assessment on the classification, stating the features and gaps of each model. The authors have categorized two types of models being discussed; the functional and conceptual models. Twenty models were reviewed and the results of the assessment become one of the foundation criteria in proposing a new records classification model.

TYPES OF MODELS

There are 20 models with two types of representations discussed in this chapter: functional and conceptual. Functional model provides graphical to support the explanation, as in function modeling (UBC project, COP, BDR, and DoD RMFI models) or conceptual/basic diagramming (FAT, records generation and types (Cook and Franks Model), MoReqs, ISO, ICA, NOARKs, UK BCS, and Australian Handbook HB5031). Fig. 4.1 illustrates the models for types discussed in this chapter.

Functional Models

Function-Activity-Transaction (Schellenberg, 1956)

The first model that becomes a foundation framework for developing function-based classification is function-activity-transaction (FAT) model proposed by Schellenberg (1956). The FAT model is based on functions,

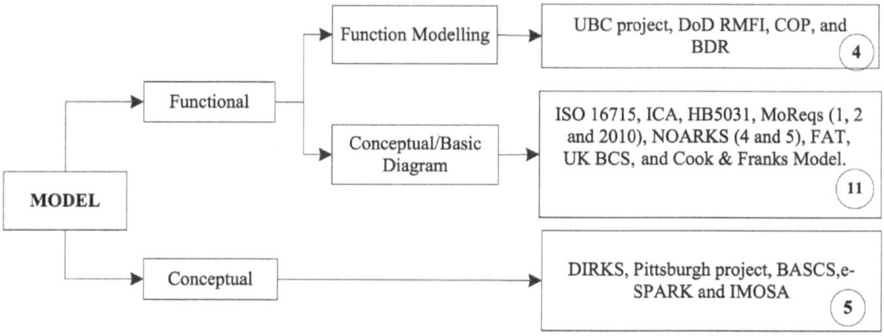

Figure 4.1 Types of models.

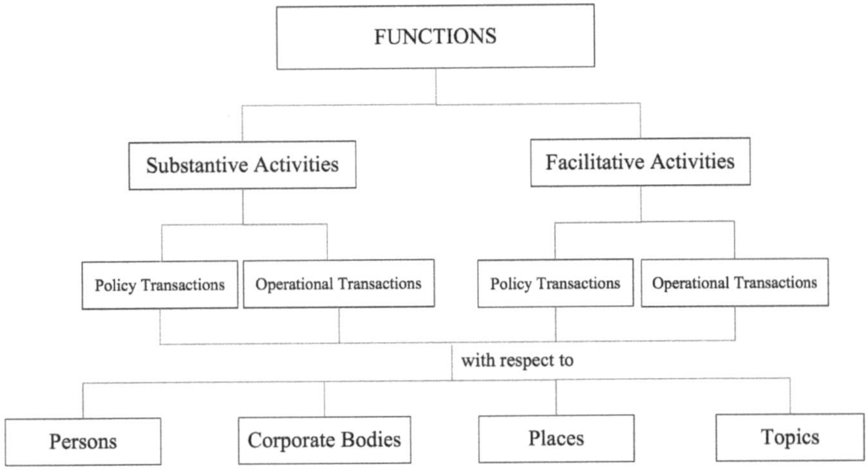

Figure 4.2 Functions-activities-transactions model.

activities, and transactions in organization. Fig. 4.2 depicts a breakdown of functions into activities and activities into transaction. The term "function" is used to cover all the responsibilities assigned to accomplish the organization's missions. It is common to base these functions on legislative requirements or organizational policies. A class of actions that will accomplish specific function is called an activity. The activity may include a number of sequential or related individual transactions.

There are three basic components to develop function-based classification system: function, activity, and transaction. These components are influenced by action, organization, and subject matter.

1. Action. Actions are defined as having a subject, verb, and purpose (Alberts, Schellinck, Eby, & Marleau, 2010). Action and function are interrelated because function is derived from a single action, while a sequence of multiple actions is called as process. Each function breaks down into a number of activities, which are in turn broken down into a number of individual transactions. There are two main types of activities, substantive and facilitative. Substantive activities relate to the technical and professional work of the organization, while facilitative activities are those related to the internal management of the organization. Activities would produce two types of transaction: policy and operational transactions. Policy transactions determine the course of action completed by all transactions of a single class, whereas, operational transactions are specific individual transactions that take place in line with policy decisions.

2. Structure of the organization. Organizational structure is related to records because records reflect it. Organizations are different from agencies. While organizations are not controlled by the government, agencies are directly under the government control. An organizational structure reflected in a classification scheme is represented by the main organizational elements of the agency as the primary class. This will only work if organizational elements are stable and well defined.
3. Subject matter. It is used by exception and only with certain kinds of records such as reference records or information files. Files are numerous and are created whenever governmental activities become specialized in relation to particular subjects or only for purposes such as reference. Subject headings are derived from subject matters to classify such records. This method is commonly used to classify library materials. Subject-based classification is not suitable for public records because of the tendency of applying a broad general scheme based on subject headings. These types of records could be more effectively arranged according to the functions of the organization.

The FAT model proposed by Schellenberg becomes a foundation framework for developing a function-based classification scheme, such as Pittsburgh electronic recordkeeping research, DoD records management functions and information (DoD RMFI) Models, and MoReqs, because of its practical application to organizations. However, the model has been debated for its practical and theoretical limitations (Yeo, 2007; Foscarini, 2009; Alberts et al., 2010).

The Preservation of the Integrity of Electronic Records (The UBC Project, 1997)

The model generated from UBC project is to define the activities for the genesis and preservation of an agency's known archival fonds. Its scope was to control records (archival documents) according to the agency's mandate using the principles of archival science. The trustworthiness of records was defined from diplomatic analysis. The life cycle of records was subscribed to maintain a clear divide between the active records phase and the archival phase. The active phase included processes of creation, classification, maintenance, use, and disposition of records. This has resulted in a metadata standard for records management application. While the archival phase catered for appraisal, arrangement, acquisition, description, preservation, and secondary (historical) use of records. Classification requirements, including developing its scheme, code, principles, and elements involved, were explained by the model narratively. The classification was based on function, with block-numeric system and represented hierarchically.

The UBC research team and the DoD reengineering team interpreted archival and diplomatic concepts using function modeling (IDEF0) to show the relationships of components involved. The models known as activity models define all the activities associated with managing records (create, handle, and preserve). The activity models consist of managing archival framework, create records, preserve records, and survey records creator. Example of the model is referred from DoD RMFI model in Fig. 4.3 because of the similarity in the core function of these models.

Department of Defense: Records Management Function and Information Models (DoD, 2003)

This model depicts an agreed process and data requirements for the creation of records throughout the United States Department of Defense (DoD). The model provides a framework for the development of activities for office automation, automated information system, and workflow systems. It is the result of collaborated efforts of experts in archival science, records managers, and automation personnel in regard to records management and technical issues.

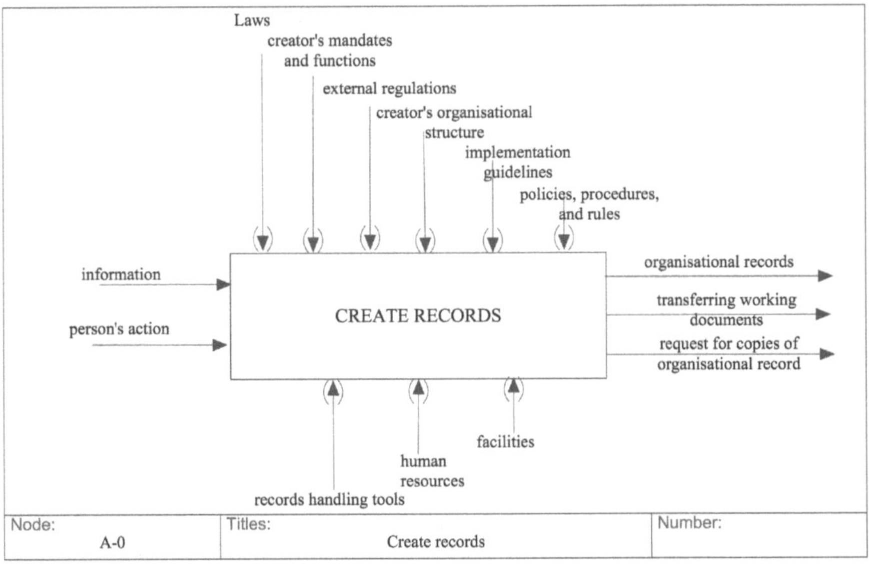

Figure 4.3 High-level function modeling of create records.

The function model was developed using the IDEF0 tool, and reflects the way records creation occurs (Fig. 4.3). The coverage of this model is detailed from a user's viewpoint and takes into consideration the facilities, human resources, and records-handling tools. In addition to this, the model also considers laws, creator's mandates and functions, external regulations, creator's organizational structure, and implementation guidelines and policies, procedures, and rules. Consequently, the model produces organizational records, transfers working documents, and receives request for copies of organizational records. All these are depicted in a function-based model for creating records.

The model, however, is limited by a discussion of the records creation by addressing only the making of records and the processes involved in maintaining working documents. The processes for making records include receiving documents, making documents, setting aside, and coding records. The processes involved in maintaining records, on the other hand, include aspects of storage, screening, and retrieving.

The naming used for classification was the "set aside" and "code records" activities. These activities occurred during creation of records. Once the information was received in the system, the system processed it in the form of a document. The document underwent classifying process for records or non-records material. If the document is classified as records, it should be coded as records by considering its disposal schedule and should be produced as organizational records. On the other hand, this model also described the process for non-records material, which need to be classified for retrieval and searching purposes.

The categories attached to this model include glossary, descriptions for relationship in the 1995 information model (did not cover in this chapter), and reader's guide to IDEF0 functions models. The details involved in classification process were not included in the model. No further explanation on classification process was covered in this project.

Evolution of Records Generation (Cook, 1992) and Records Type Functional Classification (Franks, 2013)

Records in the electronic environment have evolved from being simply machine-readable records to electronic and digital records (Fig. 4.4). The evolution of records created by technology has changed as to how the records are classified. The changes can be seen as classification is now function-based instead of subject. Records created in the 1960s were classified based on subject-based, but after 1990s, the function-based

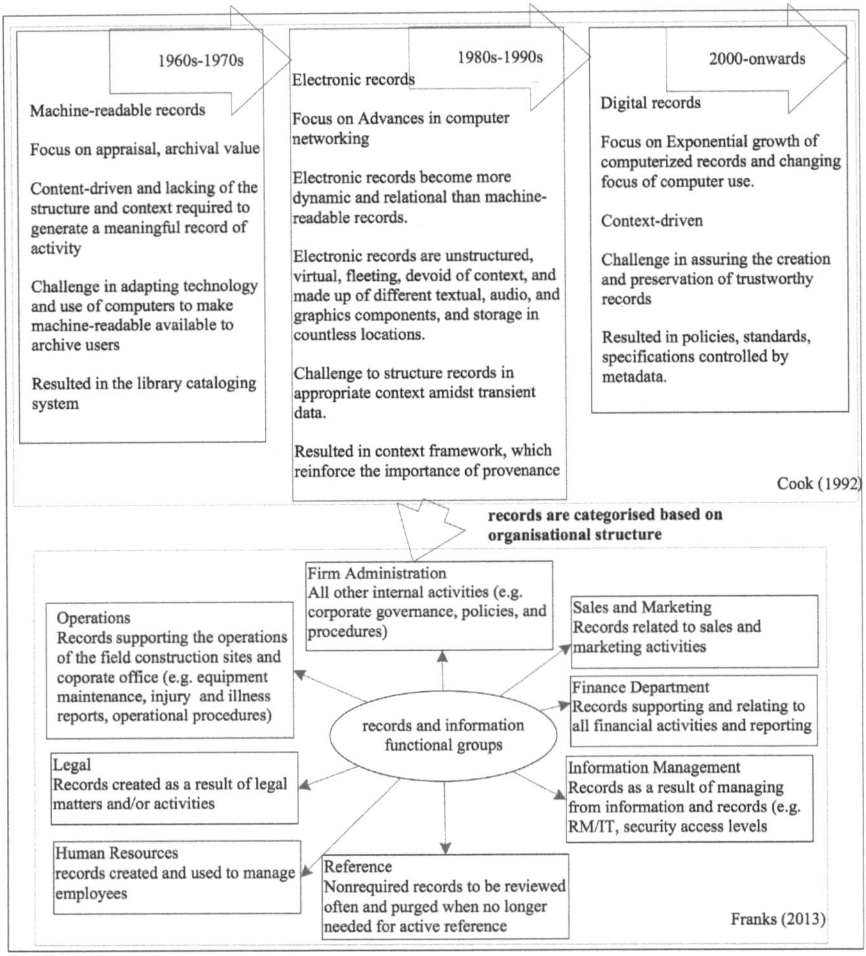

Figure 4.4 Records generation (Cook, 1992) and categorization based on organizational structure (Franks, 2013).

classification is more adopted. The function-based classification should be aligned to organizational structure, because the structure contributes to the reasons of records creation and relates to the records creator. This is the basic principle to classify records. Records classification is followed to categorize or group records into retrieval unit (Franks, 2013). Fig. 4.4 shows how generations of records evolved and how they categorized based on organization. Every department in organization has different functions. Records categorized by functions offer benefits such as understanding of the relationship between the business and its records; capability to identity records for evidential value; prioritizing records based on business value;

and facilitate retention decision and allow retention requirements at the point of creation (Franks, 2013).

Model Requirements for the Management of Electronic Records (MoReq, 2001)

The specifications for managing electronic records were designed by the European Union Council's Donnees Lisibles par Machine (DLM) Forum. Intention of the specifications is to provide both public and private organizations with a set of parameters that would ensure electronic recordkeeping systems to create, maintain, and preserve the evidence required for general operational, legal, and archival purposes. The specifications are known as model requirements for the management of electronic records (MoReq), which consist of three versions: MoReq (2001), MoReq2 (2008), and MoReq2010 (2011).

Model Requirements for the Management of Electronic Records (MoReq, 2001)

MoReq incorporates the introduction of new electronic records management systems and applications, and addresses and improves the capabilities of existing solutions. MoReq has taken traditional archival science and records management disciplines into account. These were interpreted appropriately in the electronic environments. MoReq specifications provide both functional and nonfunctional requirements designed to provide confidence and integrity in managing electronic records, by combining both the advantages of electronic ways of working with records management theory.

MoReq recommends aggregation of files to classify records in a structured manner which, if conducted with good practice, should reflect business functions. This approach is taken from a records management perspective. The representation of an aggregation is referred to as a "classification scheme," commonly represented in a hierarchical (vertical) order, but also supported by a thesaurus and horizontal order (less common). Fig. 4.5 shows an example on how classes and files were presented in basic diagram for identifying metadata elements.

MoReq had a wide scope intended to cater for European countries, which resulted in limitations for precise representations onto existing requirements without modifications. MoReq also did not cover the practical aspects of records, instead described the capabilities required for the management of electronic records by computer software. In addition, MoReq was also an intentionally user-centric design, using the type of terminology commonly used by those working with electronic records.

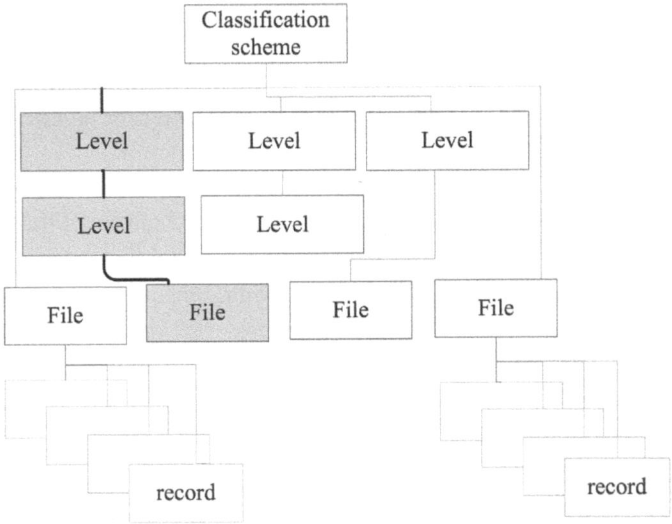

Figure 4.5 Classes and files represented in MoReq (2001).

Model Requirements for the Management of Electronic Records, Update and Extension (MoReq2, 2008)

The MoReq2 was a result of a joint effort between The National Archives of UK and the MoReq team to merge the best of both sets of requirements and pool resources to establish a common set of requirements that would benefit the vendors (Krahn, 2012). MoReq2 combined the smooth narrative and testing regime of the UK requirements with the flexibility and applicability of the original MoReq. The combination has resulted into new additional modules for:

- classification and file organization;
- ensuring access controls and security;
- enabling retention and disposition;
- capturing and declaring records;
- referencing (including system identifiers and classification codes)
- enabling search, retrieval, and display;
- system administration (audit, reporting, and review)
- much larger set of optional modules (including workflow, case management, encryption, digital rights management, and more); and
- wide range of nonfunctional requirements to meet organization-specific preferences and needs.

MoReq2 presents different classification scheme from MoReq. Fig. 4.6 depicts the classification scheme in MoReq2, which includes classes, files,

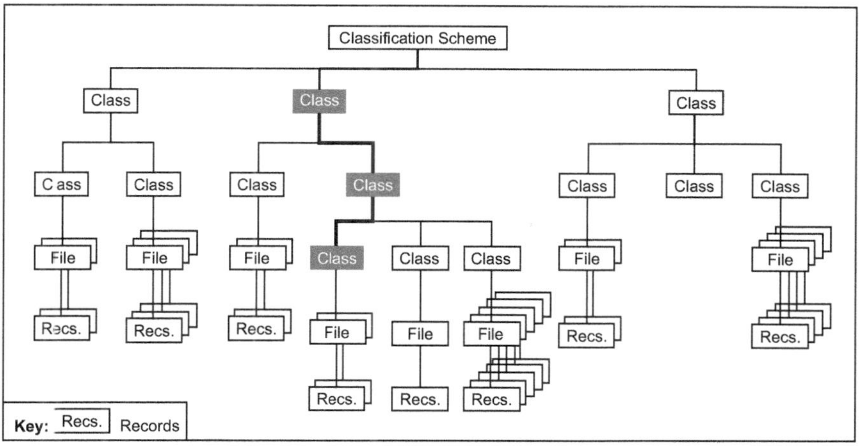

Figure 4.6 Class representation of MoReq2 classification scheme (MoReq2, 2008).

and records. In contrast, MoReq classification scheme comprised level, files, and records. The MoReq2 intended to serve as a practical tool in helping organizations meet their business needs for the management of both computer-based and paper-based records.

The main differences between MoReq and MoReq2 included the following (MoReq2, 2008):

- The language used in MoReq2 was more precise and rigorous because MoReq2 had a testing framework and a testing regime. Consequently, this version was much longer than MoReq. On the contrary, MoReq had neither.
- MoReq2 was under formal governance by the DLM Forum. MoReq was not governed.
- MoReq2 provided a roadmap for development while MoReq had neither roadmap nor development.
- MoReq2 was accompanied by an XML schema. MoReq did not. MoReq2 is modular. There is a "core" of basic recordkeeping requirements, and optional modules for functionality needed by some organizations but not others.
- MoReq2 included a metadata model that was much more complete than the model in MoReq.
- MoReq2 included many functional enhancements compared with MoReq, such as subfiles and components.

However, the enhancements in MoReq2 did not overcome the limitations in MoReq. The limitations of MoReq remained the same in MoReq2 including a wide scope, no practical aspects but only covering capabilities for managing electronic records, and being user-centric. Even though MoReq2 claimed to be an improvement over the previous specification, the launch of MoReq2 was trampled by the general global economic downturn and the rise of Microsoft's SharePoint (Lappin, 2011).

The MoReq2010 Core Services and Plug-In Modules (2011)

The MoReq2010 was introduced to tackle issues in electronic records management system (EDRMS). Among the issues in EDRMS are that the records are created and stored in many different content repositories, and these repositories may or may not have records management functions. Organizations that implement a corporate EDRMS also assume that their entire staff store records. These reasons have further affected the EDRMS implementation that was already losing its momentum (Lappin, 2011) because of the barriers such as user resistance, familiarity and comfort with paper, poor recordkeeping practices, lack of top management support, new information sharing culture such as emails, bad system design, the structure of organizations, and a lack of funding (Nguyen, Swatman, Fraunholz, & Salzman, 2009). The perceptions of EDRMS were seen differently in MoReq and MoReq2, which perceived the system as a standalone content repository. The situation worsened when the staff did not know which repository stored records management functions and which did not. Therefore, MoReq2010 casts EDRM that is capable of differentiating repositories with or without records management functions by incorporating within each separate application what the organization uses or what could sit behind those applications and manage records created within them (Lappin, 2011).

The MoReq2010 is a complete rewrite of MoReq and MoReq2. It has a potential implication for other standards because it addresses the management of electronic records in any business system. That is, records are not only stored in traditional ERMS/EDRMS applications but also extend the importance and need for recordkeeping requirements to be made available in all business systems (Warland & Lappin, 2011). MoReq2010 claimed to be more practical because it established a set of core services that could be shared by many different types of records system, which was a limitation in MoReq2.

In contrast with MoReq and MoReq2, MoReq2010 replaced the concept of the file with an aggregation as depicted in Fig. 4.6. In MoReq2, a "file" was limited to two levels of hierarchy beneath it (file/subfile/parts), while in MoReq2010, aggregations could have any number of levels in a hierarchy. The MoReq2010 "aggregation" has a different relationship to a

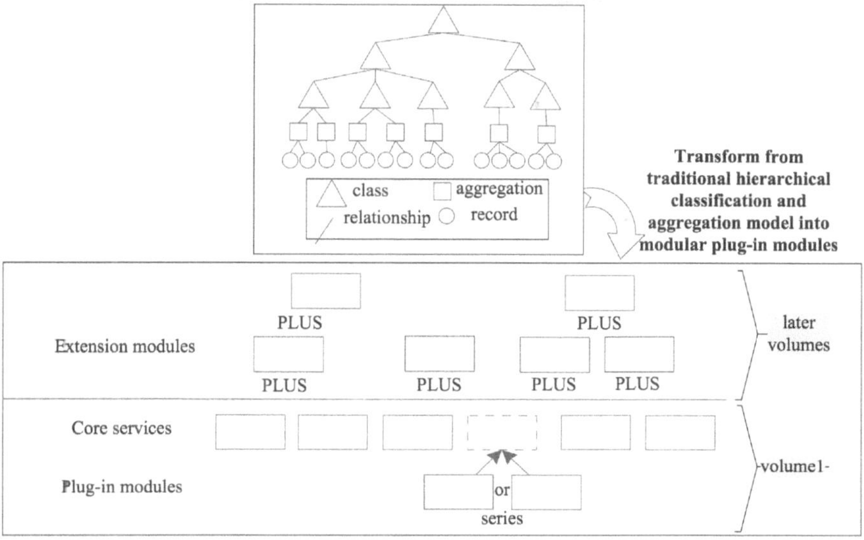

Figure 4.7 Traditional hierarchical classification and aggregation model and modular architecture MoReq2010 (2011).

business classification/file plan than a MoReq2 "file." An aggregation can be multilevel and hierarchical, and can be separated from the business classification, which can in turn be applied to determine records retention. Fig. 4.7 depicts the transformation from the traditional hierarchical model into modular architecture, which each box in the diagram represents a bundle of requirements representing either a service or a module.

MoReq2010 also allowed many classifications to be applied to records retention rules. For example, if a record is classified against more than one classification, the primary classification should be nominated for one of that record (Lappin, 2011). The primary classification is the level of classification where records inherit its retention rule from.

On the contrary, MoReq and MoReq2 adopted the concept of "one corporate business classification/file plan" that universally apply retention and access rules to all records. Only one classification could be linked to retention rules and used to apply for all records. The concept of "one specification caters for all" could also be seen when both previous MoReqs tried to specify systems that could meet the records management needs of all organization despite different sectors. The disadvantage of this concept appeared when the vendor had to configure their systems to cover all sectors and all eventualities which would be costly and less effective (Lappin, 2011). Moreover, the sustainability of the specifications was hard to maintain.

Therefore MoReq2010 claimed to be more sustainable over time as new needs can be incorporated into new modules without having to republish the whole specification.

The International Research on Permanent Authentic Records in Electronic Systems (InterPARES1, 2002; InterPARES, 2008)

The InterPARES projects which took place from 1999 to 2012 (in progress) are aimed at developing theoretical and methodological knowledge for permanent preservation of authentic, reliable, and accurate records either generated and/or maintained electronically throughout records life cycle.

There are two models derived from the project: the chain of preservation (COP) model and the business-driven recordkeeping (BDR) Model. These models covered the entire life cycle of records from creation through preservation and maintaining records' trustworthiness. The classification process is included, but is less thorough and overshadowed by other processes particularly preservation. Preservation is the main issue to be solved in this model.

The COP model is based on the perspective of the entity responsible for long-term preservation of digital records, while the BDR Model is based on the perspective of the records creating entity. The two models are mutually supportive for long-term preservation of authentic digital records and are developed based on experience through a logical construction of existing knowledge. Both models are considered as consultation drafts for preserving authentic, reliable, and accurate digital records in experiential, interactive, and dynamic systems. However, these models were not validated in the artistic and governmental sectors and needed more testing within administrative environment, by conducting walkthroughs based on the case studies.

Chain of Preservation Model (InterPARES2, 2008)

The COP model depicts all the activities and the inputs and outputs that are needed to create, manage, and preserve reliable and authentic digital records. The model was developed based on the IDEF0 modeling process using IDEF0 modeling software. IDEF0 is a US Federal Information Processing Standard for function modeling (National Institute of Standards and Technology, 1993). A function model is a structured representation of the functions, activities, and processes within the model system or subject area (IDEF, 1993).

The COP model consists of a series of diagrams to show all the activities involved in the life-cycle management of digital records, including a glossary of all the terms appearing on the diagrams. It was based on three previous models from the UBC and the InterPARES1 projects. The first model was generated from UBC project entitled "The Preservation of the Integrity of Electronic Records." The first model purported to define the activities for the genesis and preservation of an agency's archival fonds with a scope to control records according to the agency's mandate using the principles of archival science. The second and the third models were derived from InterPARES1 project, namely the Select Electronic Records Model and the Preserve Electronic Records Model. The second model defined all the activities involved in selecting authentic digital records for long-term preservation, which covered all the activities of the preserver in appraising and disposing of digital records. The third model also covered all the activities conducted in preserving authentic digital records.

The COP model was not designed to cater for classification process, but rather to the entire life cycle of records, from creation through preservation covering all the activities, and specific actions that must be undertaken to ensure the digital records are properly generated with maintained integrity and authentically reproduced at any time throughout their existence. This is due to the management of the digital records that starts from a comprehensive understanding of all phases or stages in the life cycle of records, from creation, maintenance, appraisal, disposition, to long-term preservation as authentic memorials of the actions and matters of which they are a part (InterPARES2, 2008).

Fig. 4.8 shows the high-level function modeling of the model. The COP model was based on archival concepts to produce and manage chain of preservation as the main activity. The activity is further explained as sub-activities such as managing records creation, managing records in a recordkeeping system, and preserving selected records. Each activity has its important outcomes. The first activity is to manage framework for the chain of preservation, to determine framework requirements and designing, implementing and maintaining a chain of preservation framework. A framework means all the element of policy, strategy, method, and so on, needed to manage digital records. The second activity is to manage records creation that involves overseeing and coordinating all the activities associated with managing the making and receipt of digital records and transferring created records to the recordkeeping system. The third activity involves overseeing and coordinating all the activities associated with maintaining records in the recordkeeping system to ensure their continuing authenticity, facilitating access to them, carrying out their disposition, and monitoring the overall performance of the recordkeeping system. The fourth activity involves overseeing and coordinating all the activities associated with preserving records in the permanent preservation system to ensure their continuing authenticity while in custody of the designated preserver.

The classification process occurs from the beginning of creation of records. Classification process was acknowledged for managing the records creation activity. Digital information is compiled and composed in a syntactic manner according to the specifications of the creator's documentary forms, integrated business, and documentary procedures, which resulted in documents. Documents were created from discrete aggregation of compiled digital information without being captured yet. Capture means a digital medium with fixed form and stable content to become records. Capturing process involved specifications from metadata, which are narratively included in this model's explanation. After identified documents are declared as records, the new metadata is inserted for classification process. The metadata is the classification code and register number.

Contrary to the MoReqs models, COP does not describe classification process exclusively, but rather explains the records profile needed for

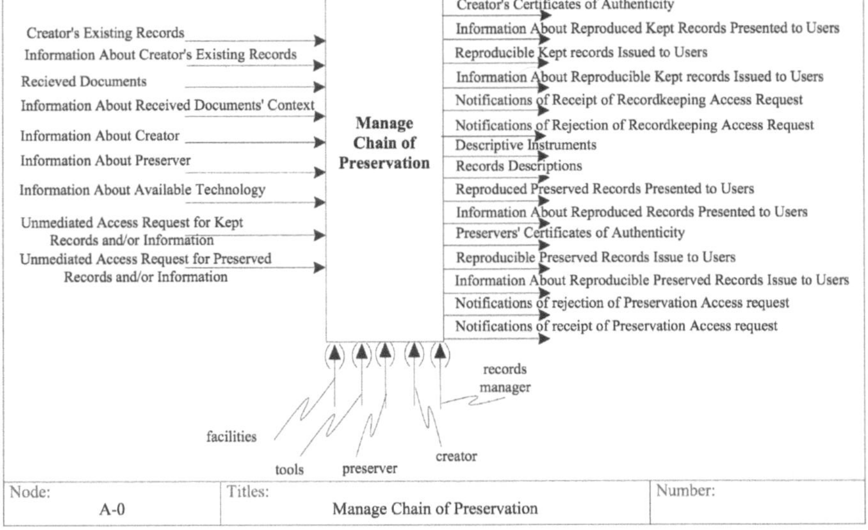

Figure 4.8 High-level function modeling of COP model.

metadata. The records profile share similar importance as classification process to ensure records integrity, authenticity, and reliability. The COP function model also does not focus on classification process exclusively, but on the whole life cycle of records. Classification process was acknowledged when making the records upon identifying inputs to classify documents to produce reports on operation of records making activity. The recordkeeping system design activity would produce a classification scheme. No further process regarding classification was described in this activity. The recordkeeping design system activity was further divided into specific activities involved, which started with development of recordkeeping scheme. The classification process was no longer mentioned for designing recordkeeping system.

Business-Driven Recordkeeping Model (InterPARES2, 2008)

The second model from InterPARES project was business-driven recordkeeping (BDR). Fig. 4.9 depicts BDR model from high-level view. The perspective of the BDR model is in the organization addressing its own business within broader juridical, economic, and cultural contexts, and the records generated by that business. The viewpoint includes both the records needed for current business and those needed to be retained and preserved for the long-term historical interests of society. The overall intent of the

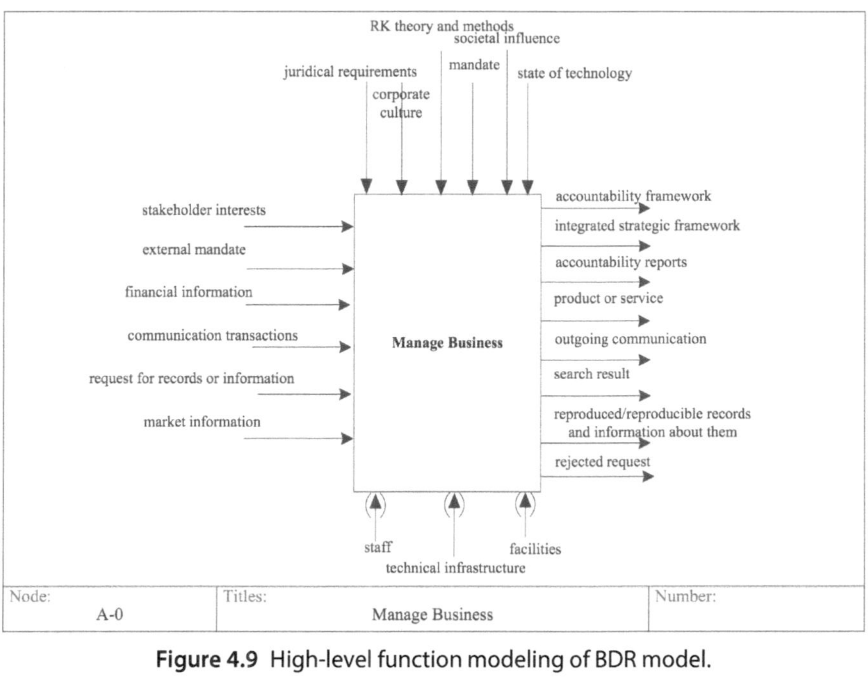

Figure 4.9 High-level function modeling of BDR model.

model is to illustrate the nexus between the needs and activities of the business of a given organization, and the records generated by those needs and activities are kept by the organization.

The BDR model offers integrated view of the business of an organization, and recordkeeping and framework for identifying the legal, juridical, ethical, business, organizational and archival requirements of specific business lines, and their juridical context. However, there was no discussion on the classification process in this model, but it works complementarily with the COP model to assist in understanding records especially from the business point of view.

Norwegian Record-Keeping System (1999–2009)

The National Archives of Norway as part of the "norsk arkivsystem" (NOARK) provide a standard for electronic records management system for Norwegian government and municipal agencies since 1984. It has been a mandatory standard since 1999, with the first to third versions (1984–1999) providing standards for registry systems, and the fourth version onward (1999) serving as an electronic records management standard including electronic archiving. The fifth version (2008) was designed to be compatible with the MoReq2 process (Berg, 2009).

Norwegian Record-Keeping System: Functional Description and Specification of Requirements (NOARK 4, 2000)

The NOARK standard was aimed at system vendors wishing to design and implement recordkeeping systems to meet the NOARK standard to be eligible for purchasing their products, and at administrative bodies seeking to purchase, develop, implement, or test a recordkeeping system meeting the NOARK 4 standard.

NOARK was based on the Pittsburgh project. The standard covered the whole of the recordkeeping system, whatever form it took and regardless of the state of activity in which the records existed as opposed to DoD 5015.2, which focused only on records management software applications for current or active records. It contained requirements for the creation, classification, maintenance, and disposition of records with the assumption that the metadata added during those activities would also consist of or at least enable the appraisal, acquisition, description, preservation, and long-term access either within the custody of the creator or to enable transfer to the custody of another preserver including archives (Norway Archives, 2002). NOARK 4 does not provide model for classification in specific, but a conceptual model for document structure and retrieval as shown in Fig. 4.10.

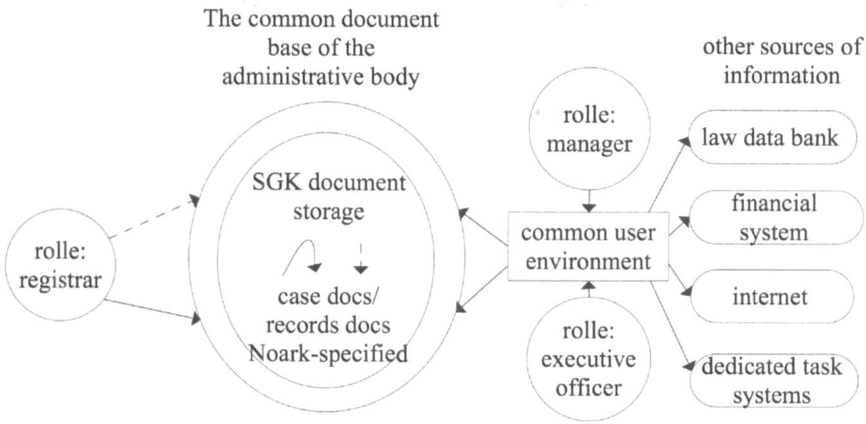

Figure 4.10 Conceptual model for document storage and retrieval (NOARK 4, 2000).

The standard was divided into two levels, functional requirements and transfer formats. It is not mandatory in Norway to implement the technical structures provided in this standard but the capacity to transfer output according to the structure defined in NOARK 4 Part 2 is mandatory. Problems with this standard became apparent when transfer processes were initiated. Data were exported in XML format, with a DTD defined for each table, which had 40–60 tables. The transfer format was basically the same as the format for exchange NOARK 4 applications. However, data in table extracts were frequently inconsistent, referential integrity rules were violated, and duplicated primary key values occurred in tables. The entire transfer model was dependent on referential integrity (Berg, 2009).

The Norwegian Record-Keeping System: Standard for Records Management (NOARK 5, 2009)

NOARK 5 began with the re-orientation of the standard to align the Norwegian national standard with the MoReq2 set of requirements. The standard specified a logical structure and included two levels of standardization for functional requirements and transfer formats. In this version, the functional requirements provided few mandatory core requirements, with optional requirements for integration and embedding in business applications.

This standard focused more on records than the applications. NOARK 5 also provided a data model that included archives, an archives group and a classification scheme depicted in Fig. 4.11. The classification scheme classed records into files, records, documents, and assigned a format for each class to be transferred as one file in a bit stream. The formats accepted were

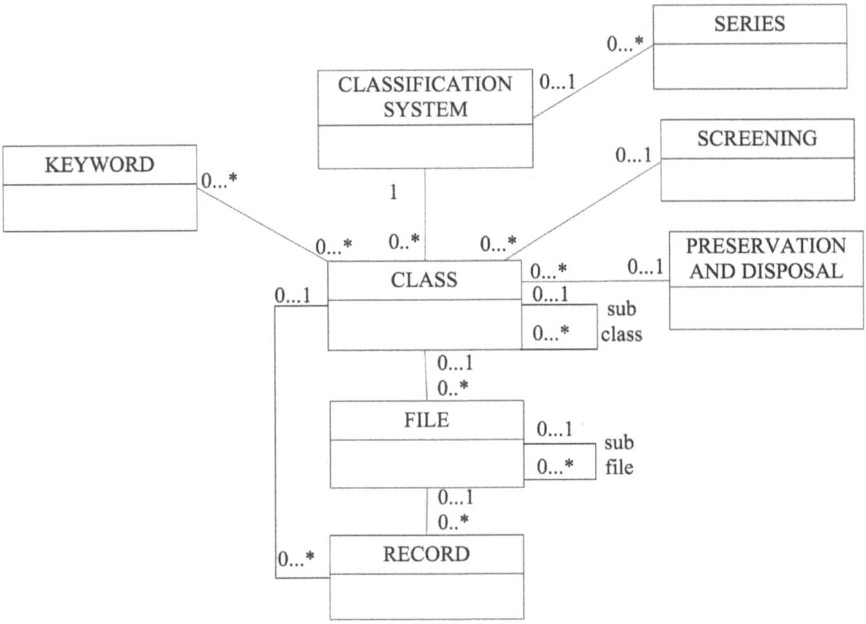

Figure 4.11 Conceptual models for records structure, fonds and series, and classification system (NOARK 5, 2009).

text (.txt), TIFF v.6, XML and PDF/A. The transfer format was radically simplified and more robust, and confined to eight archival units (metadata objects). Archival information was not confined to the technical structure but more focused on the logical structure of the records. The transferring process was also improved from the complex transfer structure in NOARK 4 into one that was less complex and with correct transfers (Berg, 2009). The model also described records from files and classes to create classification system. The system is referred from the series. Keyword, screening, preservations, and disposal processes are referred from classes.

NOARK standards version four and five focused on functional requirements and the transfer process for archival institutions. Issues arose to improve the standards including with preservation and the integrity and authenticity of records, which required organizations to maintain evidence of preserved records.

UK Business Classification Scheme Design (BCS, 2003)

This initiative was undertaken to fulfill a requirement of ISO 15489 and attempts to be a full representation of the business of an organization.

The UK Business Classification Scheme Design is a guideline to develop classification schemes from both the archival and records management perspectives. The guidelines are thorough and consist of definitions of related terminologies, intellectual control and appraisal issues, relationships between business classification scheme and technical electronic document records management, approaches to produce a business classification scheme, the main methodologies, issues with case files, and considerations for the maintenance of the business classification scheme. The guidelines are practical and can be used to complement the classification model used to describe generic aspects required to develop the model. This guideline also includes a hybrid approach for a mixed function- and subject-based approach which is more useful for managing case files. The guidelines, however, do not provide steps to develop the classification scheme, it is only a generic guideline. The basic diagramming also described function-based classification from administrative view (Fig. 4.12).

This model provides a theoretical discussion about how to manage records, which is a generic guideline, without providing instructions to develop the classification scheme. Most of the content of the model is about do's and don'ts in classifying records, and does not address how to apply the classification model. This model is useful as a foundational input; however, it does not suffice for developing a classification system.

The ICA Principles and Functional Requirements for Records in Electronic Environments and ISO 16175 - Information and Documentation - Principles and Functional Requirements for Records in Electronic Environments - Part 2: Guidelines and Functional Requirements for Digital Records Management Systems (ISO 16175, 2011)

By 2008, the National Archives of Australia (NAA) decided to collaborate with other jurisdictions that were undertaking similar efforts to produce a truly international set of model requirements for electronic records management systems (Cunningham, 2008). This was to overcome confusions in existing specifications. Thus, the NAA incorporated much of its work along with that of representatives from Asia, Africa, Europe, and North America into an effort to create a truly international set of functional requirements under the banner of the International Council of Archives (ICA). The collaboration resulted in the release of the ICA principles and functional requirements for records in electronic environments (ICA, 2008a, 2008b, 2008c) that in turn formed the basis for ISO 16175.

The ICA functional requirements were accepted as the ISO 16175-2 standard for ERMS in 2011 (ISO 16175-2, 2011). The ICA team worked closely with DLM members in the development of MoReq2 as a key stakeholder and contributor (Cunningham, 2008). The purpose of developing a standard set of requirements based on ICA was to align with MoReq2 rather than compete with it, and being less costly to implement compared with

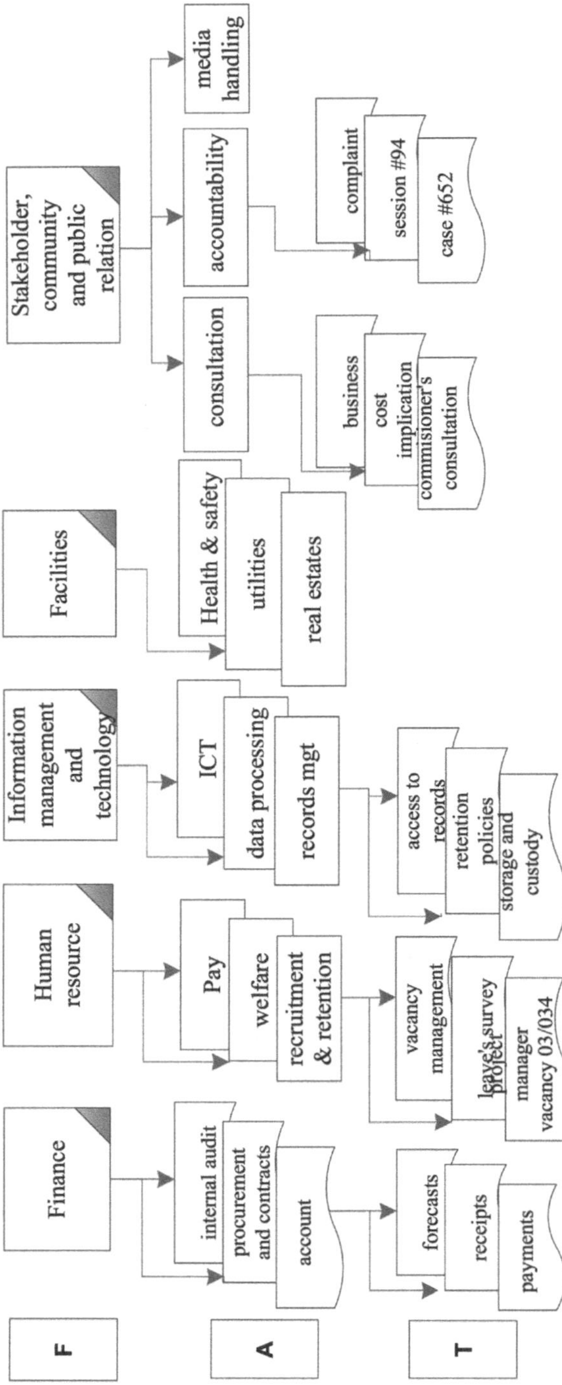

Figure 4.12 Administrative function-based structure (Todd, 2003).

models that were less specific. The development of ICA did not only refer to MoReq2 but also to functional requirements of Archives New Zealand which had already scaled down the MoReq requirements for their own 2005 release (Archives New Zealand, 2010). Therefore, the ICA standard claimed to have less daunting requirements for a diverse range of users particularly of the developing world because their statements are more principle-based, although still maintaining the essential concepts, contents, and structure of the European functional requirements as with the Pittsburgh project's original articulation (Cunningham, 2008).

With their focus on prescriptive specifications intended to enable design and testing of electronic records management systems, the emerging European and ICA/ISO functional requirements were similar enough that they were easily recognizable among the growing stable of functional requirements available (Krahn, 2012).

However, while both ICA and ISO provide functional requirements for developing electronic/digital records management systems, neither specifically outlines the requirements for records classification in detail. Both standards refer to the classification of records in conjunction with electronic/digital records management systems but not the records classification itself, such as the requirements, methods, strategies, and elements of the classification. Fig. 4.13 depicts how aggregation of records is described, but the diagram is only at a conceptual level.

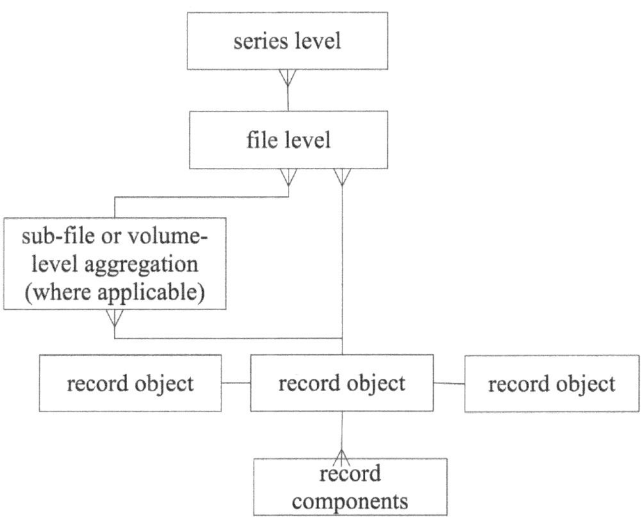

Figure 4.13 Aggregation of records (ICA, 2008a, 2008b, 2008c).

The Australian Handbook Classification (HB 5031, 2011)

There are four key concepts of records classifications: records titling, metadata, current design, and other factors as shown in Fig. 4.14.

The Australian Handbook discusses classification in detail and includes graphical representations to describe hierarchical model schemes. It covers a number of areas including: records titling; classification design such as monolingual thesaurus construction; facet analysis and work process analysis; and classification elements.

The broad and generic coverage of the handbook is handy for the novice developer, especially one with no background in the records management

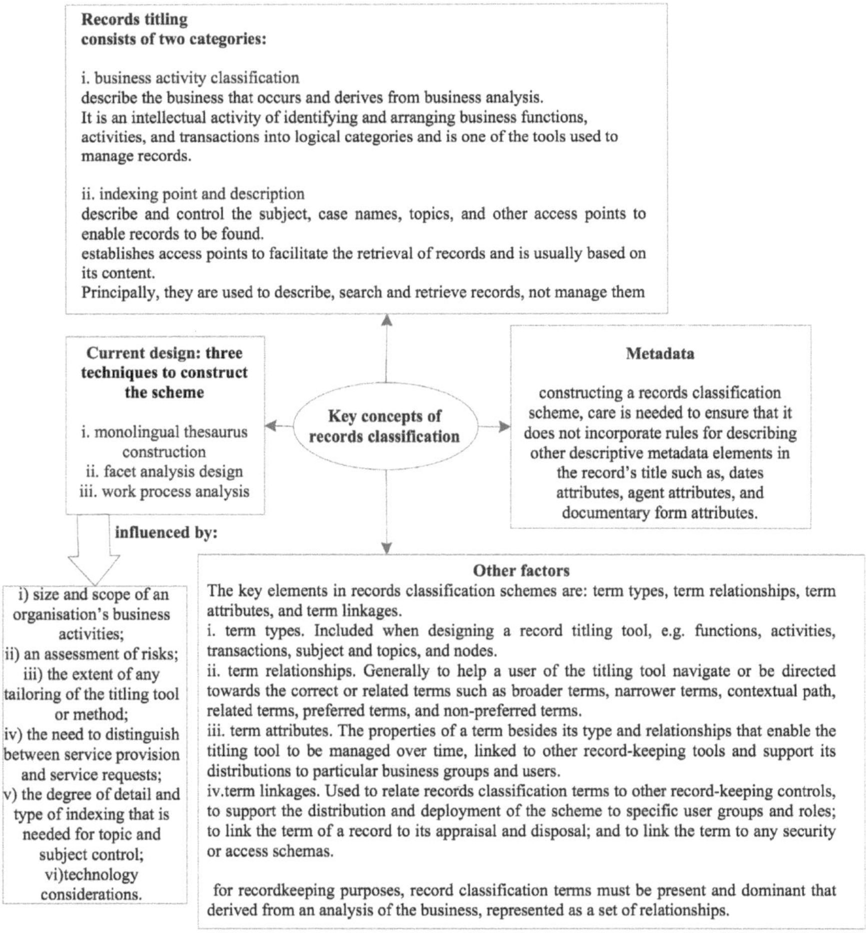

Figure 4.14 Key concepts of records classification (HB 5031, 2011).

field. However, the handbook does not provide details of the processes involved from the higher level to the lower level of classification.

Monolingual Thesaurus Construction

The first technique has been adopted extensively in the library sciences. In brief, this method lists a complex set of related business functions and activities. It incorporates a set of topics, subjects within a single hierarchical structure, and can be transformed into an alphabetical list that includes definitions, cross references, and relationships. The hierarchical presentation is referred to as the "business classification scheme," while the alphabetical representation is referred to as a "thesaurus." Fig. 4.15 shows the model applied to the technique of single hierarchical records classification scheme.

However, this technique is not widely recognized, not well known, and attracts controversy if adopted. The pitfall of this method arises when it comes to distinguish between tools designed to retrieve document content and tools designed to manage records. This is because some techniques of this design do not conform to the standards of recordkeeping for managing records but are based more on finding content and retrieval. Moreover, the technique includes repetitive reminders to users that it is not a series of subject headings and the vocabulary control is not the main context.

Facet Analysis Design

The second technique is facet analysis design that is widely used by information professionals to define categories of descriptions that can be applied to resources. It seeks to divide and describe the information into its

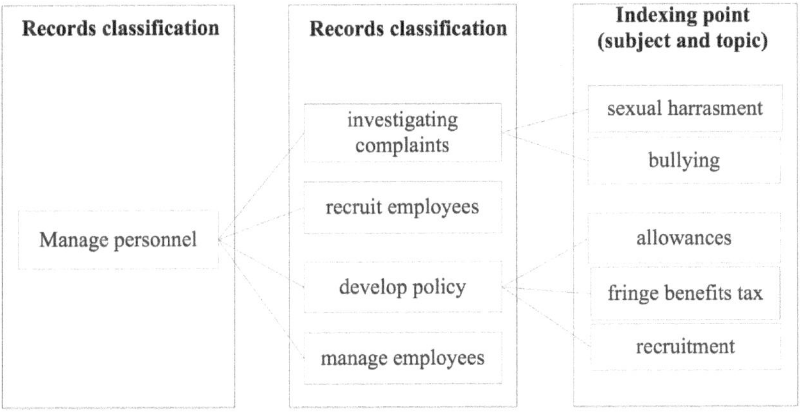

Figure 4.15 Simple, single hierarchical records classification scheme model (HB 5031, 2011).

characteristic categories. The technique is called facet analysis because each characteristic division is known as a facet. Faceted analysis is common in website design as it provides users with multiple points to search, view, and navigate to records (HB 5013, 2011; Broughton, 2010).

This technique allows the developer to define a series of mutually exclusive categories that can be applied to a resource (e.g., people, organization, and topic). These facets can be linked together to describe topical and subject-based retrieval points. The use of facets for recordkeeping purposes is often in the form of encoding schemes deployed as individual metadata elements and values, and documented in the subject element of metadata schemas that can then be used to define multiple presentation views, independent titling tools, and independent but linked lists of records classification terms.

The study finds that this method is now very common with a major increase in use over the last 15 years especially within the field of library science where it was first formalized (Broughton, 2010). Most LIS subject indexing tools (classifications, subject heading lists, and thesauri) now demonstrate features of facet analysis to a greater or lesser degree (Broughton, 2010). Fig. 4.16 depicts the model of multiple hierarchical/facet analysis records classification.

Work Process Analysis

The third model uses the work process analysis technique, which is a detailed records classification scheme design method. The technique identifies business analysis and workflow that involves taking the broad function and activity terms in a business classification scheme. The identification and analysis of work process is conducted to pinpoint requirements and logical aggregations of records.

Figure 4.16 Multiple hierarchical records classification scheme model (HB 5031, 2011).

The technique can be incorporated into the design and configuration of business systems that manage records, workflow management system that route records and documents, and content management systems that store records. However, the technique does not rely on placing records within structured folders in order to preserve the relationships between the records classification and the records, but it preserves the relationships between the records classification scheme and records as separate metadata elements of function, activity, and transaction, or aggregation via workflow that is directly applied to a record.

Therefore, with the granularity of description incorporated into the records classification scheme, using this method enables the scheme to be linked to routine and standard work processes using a rules-based approach which eventually offers great implementation options including: (1) linking together to form a continuous records of activity using relationship rather than folder and file plans; (2) exposing detail of the work being performed; (3) linking to and distributing work to the appropriate actors; (4) linking work processes; (5) enabling access and security; and (6) incorporating records classification scheme within business system.

This technique is more rigorous and complicated than monolingual thesaurus construction and facet analysis design, therefore, it is more useful to organizations to develop records classification into EDRMS; incorporate internal and external records creation requirements into the scheme; and manage and link work processes, exclusive indexing points, and encoding schemes for facets (HB 5031, 2011). Fig. 4.17 shows the model of records classification scheme that derives from work process analysis.

The records classification scheme is commonly applied to records captured and controlled in an electronic document and records management system. This tool uses the scheme to title the folder (or records aggregation) so that the records contained within inherit the classification attribute from the container rather than applying the classification directly to the records. Records classification scheme can embed attributes directly onto records using techniques other than inheritance from a folder. For instance, it can inherit them from an aggregation in a workflow as an attribute attached to a documentary form, or inherit them from a business system or collaboration space. Although records classification can be applied to records stored in a business system, this system rarely manages records using folders or files, therefore, a records classification scheme that incorporates transactions is more suitable for managing these records.

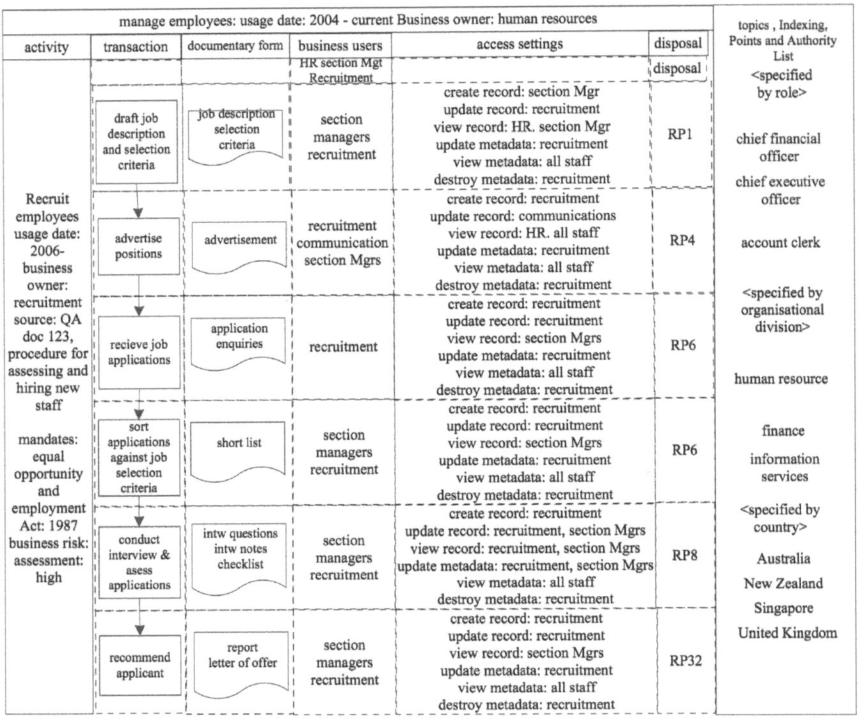

Figure 4.17 Detailed records classification scheme (HB 5013, 2011).

The Australian Records Classification model describes the concepts, elements, and models involved when developing a records classification scheme. It also explains how to gather information needed to construct the scheme. The limitation of this model is lacking an explanation of list of related standards, acts, laws, or legal requirements, and examples of records classification scheme construction. Descriptions provided in this model are foundation, abstract, and generic and do not conform to specific records types or business activities. Nonetheless, it provides a good explanation of the fundamentals of a records classification scheme, which should be better communicated across the records keeping world.

Conceptual Models

The second type of model is conceptual. Conceptual models contain lengthy textual explanation. The explanations are made narratively without any graphical presentation.

Information Management and Office Systems Advancement (McDonald, 1995)

The results from Information Management and Office Systems Advancement (IMOSA) project were divided into three phases: phase one was the prototype application based on existing functional requirements, phase two was the corporate information management information (CIMA) requirements, and the phase three discussed the current issues regarding CIMA requirements.

The prototype application offered functions such as filing, submitting, retrieving and searching, editing corporate documents, records management, the ability to verify documents, document classification to support preservation, and the ability to make available the related government's corporate memory with long-term archival value. However, retention and disposition did not feature in this prototype.

The prototype application made use of subject-based classification, automated to maintain links between hard copy and electronic holdings. The electronic holdings included documents created using various software available on the local area network. The file classification index was fully automated by using keywords from the subject field or section titles, allowing users to classify documents regardless of their knowledge of the classification system. The design of the classification system was based on the block-numeric system. The block-numeric system is a hierarchical classification system, which means each subject or function in the classification system is placed in a hierarchy, relative to other subjects or functions in the system. Broader subjects or functions are placed at the top of the hierarchy, while more specific subjects or functions are placed at a lower level. The second and third phases did not discuss the classification, therefore leaving the explanations similar to the phase one.

The University of Pittsburgh Electronic Record-Keeping Research Project (The Pittsburgh Project, 1997)

The University of Pittsburgh Electronic Record-Keeping Research Project (Pittsburgh project) has established a model for developing functional requirements and metadata specifications based on warrant, defined as the laws, regulations, best practices, and customs that regulate recordkeeping (Cox & Duff, 1997). Warrant could be identified from studying patterns within the recordkeeping practices of high-risk, real-world sectors to establish and isolate the functional requirements that enabled those sectors to enjoy legal and regulatory reliance on their own electronic records.

The functional requirements focused on the methods to maintain records' integrity, reliability, and authenticity to ensure the evidence of records are protected. Records as evidence provide internal accountability for organizations, and make it possible to determine what was done in the past. The integrity and reliability of records were determined from the interrelationship between the form, structure, and authorship of documents (Duranti, 1998). The authenticity of records is also important to ensure records can be suitable as evidence, and can be evaluated from diplomatics analysis.

There is no classification process in the proposed requirements. However, the requirements provide a specification needed to ensure the preservation of evidence in electronic form and not the application requirements for archival or records management systems. This Pittsburg requirement contributed as a methodology reference to develop requirements for preservation. Fedora and the Preservation of University Records Project (2006) revealed no references were made from Pittsburgh requirement for the classification section, but referred to MoReqs, DoD 5015.2, Indiana requirements, and PRO requirements.

The influence of the project is evident in other projects such as Indiana University's Electronic Records Project, the Norwegian Record-Keeping System: Functional Description and Specification of Requirements (NOARK 4), the Norwegian Record-keeping System: Standard for Records Management (NOARK 5), the United Kingdom-Functional Requirements, the Model Requirements for the Management of Electronic Records, Update and Extension, International Council of Archives' Principles and Functional Requirements for Records in Electronic Environments, ISO 16175 Information and Documentation – Principles and Functional Requirements for Records in Electronic Environments – Part 2: Guidelines and Functional Requirements for Digital Records Management Systems, and Information Management and Office Systems Advancement (IMOSA).

Electronic Records Management Software Applications Design Criteria Standard (US Department of Defense, 2007).

The DoD 5015.2 standard established a minimum set of baseline functional requirements necessary for all records management applications used within the Department of Defense. The baseline functional requirements were set for classified marking, access control, and other processes, and identified nonmandatory features desirable for records management application software. It aimed to ensure that records management applications were capable of meeting the recordkeeping requirements of the DoD throughout their information life cycle such as create, distribute, use, and maintain.

Although the standard provided the foundations for developing records management applications from both the IT and records management perspectives, from the viewpoint of practitioner the standard was considered to be irrelevant, obsolete, over-engineered, or unnecessary for managing information at maintenance phase. Lueders (2013) believed that documents and records could not be distinguished because all the material in the system would be discoverable evidence in a legal matter. Because unstructured electronic content cannot be segmented in records or documents, this could cause incalculable damage to the content management industry. Moreover, the processes, procedures, roles, and permissions are all designed to meet the specific requirements for records management functionality in a DoD repository. In this respect, the 5015.2 more closely resembles a solution requirements document than an application standard, which should define solutions to problems experienced by an entire market, not one particular customer. But vendors were forced to meet every requirement in the standard or risk failing certification.

On the other hand, the standard integrated requirements for the creation and maintenance of a reliable electronic record to protect the authenticity, reliability, and integrity of records. This requirement was generated by the UBC project with specific DoD directives, policies, guidelines, and procedures as well as applicable executive orders, national and international standards, codes, and regulations. Once researchers had established the DoD's recordkeeping requirements (for active records) they were able to graphically express them using integrated definition for function (IDEF) modeling technique already employed by the UBC project. This can be seen in the Chain of Preservation model by InterPARES2.

Electronic Strategy for Preservation of Government Records and Archives (e-SPARK, 2008)

E-SPARK (e-Strategy for Preservation of Government Records and Archives) is a special research project supported by the highest authority in Malaysia designed to promote good records keeping across the entire public sector. Its implementation was carried out in two phases. The first phase concentrated on the preparation of working tools such as guidelines, procedures, and system specifications. The second phase was dedicated to system development and system integration—ERMS (electronic records management systems) and AMS (archival management systems) (Shafie, 2007).

This model contains guidelines for storing and preserving electronic records or data in the Malaysian public sector. This is in relation to their evaluation, segregation, storage, transfer, preservation, and security. The guidelines are meant for records officers, heads of IT, information system officer and personnel assigned to deal with electronic records and data management in their departments.

Designing and Implementing Record-Keeping Systems (DIRKS-Australia) and Business Activity Structure Classification System (BASCS-Canada)

Designing and implementing recordkeeping systems (DIRKS) is a method used to develop a business classification scheme (BCS). It is "a conceptual model showing an organization's functions, activities, and transactions in a hierarchical relationship and the analysis of the organization's business activities and processes" (DIRKS 2006a, 2006b, 2006c). It is a "logical model" that archivists, or whoever in the organization is responsible for the relevant function, draw on to design "classification tools for records management." Therefore, the BCS is not in itself a records classification tool, although the difference between that and a records classification scheme or a thesaurus (which is considered equivalent by NAA) would only emerge at the transaction level, i.e., at the point where records may be created. In practice, the methodology recommends the translation of functional terms of the BCS into "topics and/or subtopics" to serve the "purpose of records classification ... [that is,] to title the record for searching and retrieval." Like Schellenberg, this approach appears to state that the primary purpose of classification is records retrieval. It ignores the more substantial need to be explicit and fix the relationships among records in series and files (Xie, 2007).

The Australian BCS model is the result of a simple, but well-articulated, functional analysis process. It is close to the Canadian model.The difference is in its wider focus, as BCS incorporates investigation of the broader social context, or an "ambient function" that an organization's goals and strategies depend on. It suggests that contents can be attributed to topics at the lower level of the classification. These contents could be records type, subject-matter, transaction, the output of a small group of tasks, and so on.

However, BSC model has its drawbacks such as the definition of functional term; failure to acknowledge the existence of other type of functions besides those that are structured, sequential, and routinized; the exclusion of the discussion on classification design on examination of existing records, files, or recordkeeping procedures until later in the methodology; no indication to conduct complex analysis of the wider environment of recordkeeping; and no elaborations on how to adapt the conceptual representation of business processes into a workable records classification tool, in response to the requirements of the records creators.

Records classification design and thesaurus building are, in the DIRKS Manual, treated in the same way. Organizations, it is expressly said, are free to choose, according to their retrieval preferences and needs, between the hierarchical structure of a "Records Classification Scheme" and the flat, alphabetical structure of a "Functional Thesaurus." The thesaurus acts in a sense as an index to the BCS, which is the source of both records classification and thesaurus, and offers more powerful retrieval capabilities because of its flexible approach. However, the real issue that arises, according to Bedford and Morelli, 2006, is that only a hierarchical classification can serve properly the purposes of records management and achieve the objective of revealing the functional context of the records. That is, a records classification scheme must only display meaningful hierarchical trees of functional terms (Reed, 2008). Therefore, the records classification appears to be a hybrid tool in comparison to the purely functional BCS. Discussion about this BCS method appears to be primarily around information retrieval capabilities, which is not really at the core of the archival discourse.

On the other hand, the Canadian business activity structure classification system (BASCS) is a methodology for constructing function-based classification systems developed and promoted by the Library and Archives of Canada for the purpose of constructing function-based classification system to replace its subject block-numeric classification system, which has been in use for decades (Xie, 2007). It was influenced from the macro-appraisal methodology and structural-functional analysis, for assessing the value of records (Sabourin, 2001). The methodology includes extensive discussion of benefits, methodological background, implementation guidelines, and models for both operational functions and common administrative functions. However, the explanations contained in the documentation lack clarity and it is advisable to clearly set boundaries for each function to make them sensible and easier to develop the system (Xie, 2007).

CONCLUSION

The concept of classification was introduced as early as 1898 in the Dutch Manual known as "arrangement," which Jenkinson referred to as "placing." The term was coined by Schellenberg upon introducing modern archives for managing documents, which later on led to the introduction of "selection process concept" known as classification.

The process of classification evolved from being subject-based, used in the library science field t, to function-based classification in records management field. Function-based classification was introduced with the belief that records are by-products of actions, and actions were created within functions. Function-based classification is more stable and rarely changes. The theory of function-based classification has been well accepted in the US and Australia. Many projects have applied such an approach particularly BASCS, DIRKS, UK Business Classification, and Pittsburgh Project.

The 20 models reviewed here are based on classification in general, and by function in specific. Function-based classification is related with logical arrangement of all records documenting or evidencing the activities of an organization by analyzing its business functions, subfunctions, and activities. These models were described from the view of records management processes beginning with creation through preservation. Records, especially the electronic ones have a continuum life cycle and classification is conducted during the active phase.

The models discussed in this chapter take the form of concepts, guidelines, functional requirements, methodology, function models, standards with the majority are functional requirements (IMOSA, Pittsburgh project, UBC project, NOARKS, MoReqs, ICA, e-SPARK, and ISO 16175). Functional requirements capture and specify the specific intended behavior of the system being developed by defining things such as system calculations, data manipulation and processing, user interface and interaction with the application, and other specific functionality that show how user requirements are satisfied. The ICA and ISO 16175 are also standards for records management and recordkeeping. Projects like Pittsburgh and UBC produced methodologies for designing recordkeeping standards and functional requirements. A methodology means system of methods used in a particular area of study or activity (Oxford Online), or the analysis of the principles or procedures of inquiry in a particular field (Merriam-Webster Online).

Each of the models reviewed has its own strengths and limitations. Such characteristics are taken into consideration in proposing a new model to be used by organizations in Malaysia. The proposed functional model can be understood by both the records management and information technology professionals by using function modeling. The principles of classification are based on records management which is a core foundation to provide a systematic management. The principles are designed into a function modeling for IT reference.

The findings from the models' review will be used for model development in Chapter Five.

CHAPTER FIVE

The Records Classification Functional Model

INTRODUCTION

Classification is the arrangement of information items into manageable and logical categories. Records classification is different from library classification used to process information (Pearce-Moses & Davis, 2008). Librarians classify materials by subject from many different sources into a single system, collecting related materials together for convenient access. On the contrary, records managers do not reorganize records, but maintain the original order abiding by the theories of provenance and *respect des fonds*. Such an approach ensures that the evidentiary value of records is preserved and the structure or functions of records remain intact.

Therefore, the authors adopt records classification because, as suggested by Orr (2005), the National Archives of Australia (2008), and Mitchell (2003), it is more stable compared to subject-based classification. Function-based classification could also ease the process of classification and retrieval (Library and Archives Canada, 2006a). Moreover, function-based classification provides context for records rather than content (ISO 15,489, 2001; Library of Archives Canada, 2006a,b; National Archives of Australia, 2003; Robinson, 1999; Shepherd & Yeo, 2003). Function-based classification could aid appraisal and disposal activities and support the proactive management of records (Bantin, 2001; National Archives of Australia, 2003).

This chapter discusses a functional model for records classification and the explanation of each process involved. Records classification is the recognition, identification, application, and arrangement of records, based on logical and consistent criteria, within distinct functions (Guercio, 2002). The main elements to be considered in classifying records are function, action, and organizational structure (Alberts, Schellinck, Eby, & Marleau, 2010; Schellenberg, 1956). The action element is the foremost one to be considered since most records are by-products of actions and fall into groups that relate to those actions. Actions are synonymous with activities in models

Records Classification: Concepts, Principles and Methods
ISBN 978-0-08-102238-2
http://dx.doi.org/10.1016/B978-0-08-102238-2.00005-6

that refer to functions, activities, transactions, and processes (Alberts et al., 2010). This chapter also explains on electronic records management system to understand its characteristics.

DEVELOPING THE RECORDS CLASSIFICATION MODEL

Functional model is a structured system, which comprises of well-developed and well-used methods and techniques (Hughes, 2000) methods and techniques. The modeling is carried out from the perspective of data or records moving through the system (DeMarco, 1979). This approach is analytical and was employed many times, such as in Phase II Indiana Project and InterPARES Project. This model is developed by using functional modeling because it is an activity of developing models of devices, products, and processes based on component's and subcomponent's functionalities (Erden et al., 2008). According to Taylor, Medvidovic, and Dashofy (2010), functional aspects relate to what a system does, while modeling is a process activity of creating models. Functional modeling is a tool that allows a team or an individual to produce a behavioral/operational model of an existing or planned system. The resulting model shows the system functionality and the logical interconnections between that functionality. In essence, it describes how the system functionality has to cooperate to deliver the operational requirements by representing knowledge about function (Burge, 2011; Erden et al., 2008).

Functional modeling consists of diagramming, information hiding, and abstraction. First, diagram is used to represent functions because it is good at conveying the structure. Furthermore, natural languages are ambiguous and the use of textual methods to convey complex information will lead to errors. Second, the diagram presents a hierarchical form, with the highest level focusing on the essential information and the lower level explaining the fine details. The information hidden at the higher level can be revealed in lower level diagrams. Third, abstraction is referred to the diagramming convention.

The process for functional modeling begins with collecting and generating information about the system of interest. The information can be collected through data collection method such as questionnaires, interviews, discussions, observations, and document analysis. The functions related are identified, and drawn into a diagram, which becomes a flow diagram. The dictionary and specifications for the functions are compiled and generated to be included in the system model draft. These processes are done by iteration until the draft represents the real-world activities.

A model is a substitute for a real system, used when it is easier to work with a substitute than the actual system (Ford, 2009). A model is more abstract than the system it represents, eliminates unnecessary details, and focuses on the most important or relevant elements within the system (Hillston, 2003). The model presented in this chapter was developed taking both records management principles and archival science theory into consideration. Records management principles are focused on the management of current records from creation to maintenance. The primary purpose of records management is to help organizations organize records for retrieval and storage, and to protect them from misuse. Since this study focuses on classification and its application to current records, the records management principles of *respect des fonds* and provenance are noted, along with a brief reference to archival science theory. Examples of other studies that adopted the same theoretical foundation are Orr (2005); Xie (2007); Foscarini (2009); and Krahn (2012).

The proposed model later referred to as the records classification model (RCM), focuses on the first phase of recordkeeping functional requirements, called "Create" when classification process begins at the creation level. This book does not discuss the other three phases, namely "Maintain," "Disseminate," and "Administer." The main concern while creating records, from the records management perspective, is to ensure that records are created in context by ensuring its metadata, management of aggregations, and classification tools. The creation of records requires a disposition schedule; capture methods, metadata elements, forms and structure, and technology solutions. Records are controlled through processes such as registration, classification, selection, access rules, authorized use, disposition, transfer, removing, destruction, and administration of records systems. Therefore, the classification of records occurs at the "Create" phase, which is the focal interest of the authors.

A number of existing resources can be used to guide good records management. These include ICA, MoReqs, and InterPARES, all of which address the management of records from creation to disposal. None of these resources includes a method to conduct functional modeling, and none focuses solely on the classification of records. Therefore, a new model is proposed for the following reasons:

- To date, there is no model for the classification of records in Malaysia.
- There is a need to classify records in Malaysia by function. Records should not be classified based on theme, subjects, time, or place since they are not arbitrarily collected, but acquired and described in context of natural relationship between the creator and its creation (Cook, 2007).

Moreover, the classification of records by function has been widely adopted by many countries including the United States, Canada, UK, New Zealand, Australia, China, and Malaysia (paper records only).

The development of the proposed model (RCM) was achieved using a tool (IDEF0) that consists of node index, context diagrams, and decomposed diagrams. IDEF0 was used for the DoD RMFI models and the development of a model in COP/BDR. The RCM is a foundation guideline designed to identify functions in organizations for the purpose of classifying records. It is not a classification scheme; however, the development of a classification scheme can be referred from this model.

INTEGRATION DEFINITION FOR FUNCTION MODELING

IDEF0 was used to produce a functional model of the RCM. A functional model is a structured representation of the functions and activities within the modeled system or subject area (Federal Information Processing Standards Publications 183 1993). The model was developed using the *Concept Draw PRO* software. The IDEF0 model has been constructed level by level, beginning with the node index, followed by the context diagram (A-0). Levels are then decomposed to more detail diagrams (A0, A1, and A2).

IDEF0 consists of inputs, controls/constraints, outputs, and mechanisms (ICOMs). Definitions for these terms are provided by IDEF (1993).

- Input is defined as information or objects that originate outside the main activity being modeled and result in output or the outcomes of an activity. Activities have control/constraint on processes.
- Control/constraint is a form of input, seldom changing, and may direct or affect activities associated with a process.
- Mechanisms are the resources and tools required to complete the process.

IDEF0 was derived from a well-established graphical language, the structured analysis and design technique (SADT). The United States Air Force commissioned the developers of SADT to develop a function modeling method for analyzing and communicating the functional perspective of a system. IDEF0 can be used to model a wide variety of automated and nonautomated systems. For new systems, IDEF0 can be used first to define the requirements and specify the functions, and then to design an implementation that meets the requirements and performs the functions. For existing systems, IDEF0 can be used to analyze the functions the system performs and to record the mechanisms by which these are done. IDEF0 has the following characteristics, which are the reasons to use it in this study (Computer Systems Laboratory of the National Institute of Standards and Technology, 1993):

1. It is comprehensive and expressive, capable of graphically representing a wide variety of business, manufacturing, and other types of enterprise operations to any level of detail.
2. It is a coherent and simple language, providing for rigorous and precise expression, and promoting consistency of usage and interpretation.
3. It enhances communication between system analysts, developers, and users through ease of learning and emphasizing hierarchical exposition of detail.
4. It is well tested and proven, through many years of use in air force and other government development projects and private industry.
5. It can be generated by a variety of computer graphics tools; numerous commercial products specifically support development and analysis of IDEF0 diagrams and models.

NODE INDEX FOR THE DESIGN OF A RECORDS CLASSIFICATION MODEL

The development of the RCM begins with constructing a node index. A node index is used as a guide or index to list the related functions, which are then drawn in the context diagram. The context diagram is the highest level diagram and is made up of all ICMOs. In the IDEF0 model, these four components are used to represent all related activities or components involved in the model. The context diagram is decomposed to lower level diagrams, to provide detail for the processes involved. The node index provides a quick index for locating details within the hierarchical structure of diagrams as shown in Fig. 5.1.

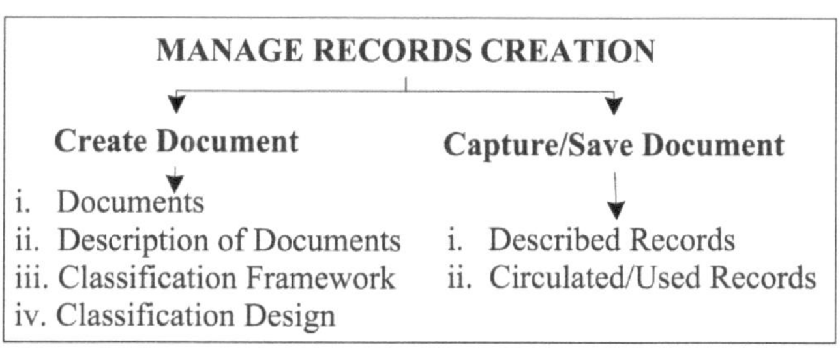

Figure 5.1 The node index.

Fig. 5.1 depicts a proposed model that consists of two core processes involved in classifying records: (1) create documents and (2) capture/save documents. The first process is document creation. The attributes of a document are composed of records elements derived from archival science theory and constructed using IT tools to become electronic documents or records. The first process produces outputs including classification framework and design. This is because the process of classification should occur when documents are created. The second process is about capturing and saving documents into the system to describe them as records and circulate them for use.

DESCRIPTION OF RECORDS CLASSIFICATION MODEL

Context Diagram for Records Classification Model

The node index is a simple way to portray the processes (referred to as "create" and "capture/save") that are incorporated in the "Manage Records Creation" element. After the node index is identified, a context diagram is drawn using the software *Concept Draw Pro*. All system functions lie within the single box shown in diagram A-0 as shown in Fig. 5.2, bounding the context of the system. Diagram A-0 describes the subject of the model and its overall context represented in a single box with its bounding arrows. The bounding arrows represent the model's ICOMs.

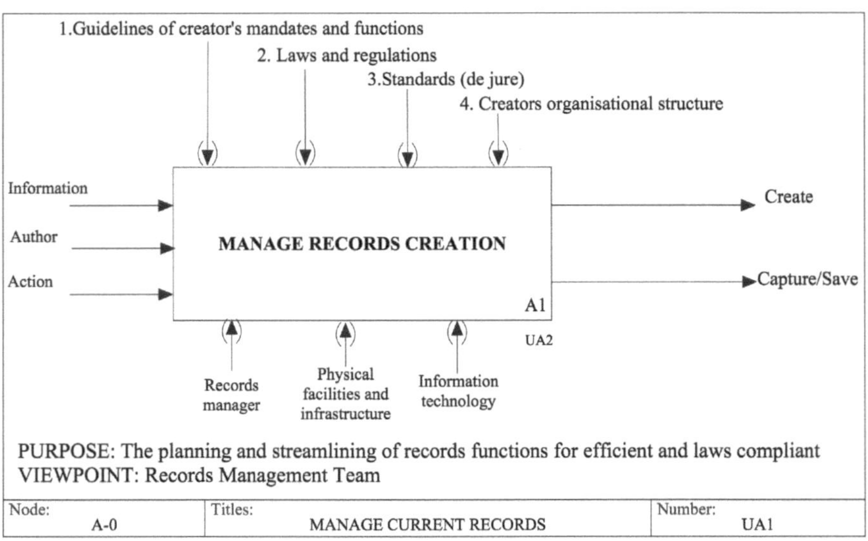

Figure 5.2 Context diagram (A-0).

Diagram A-0 decomposes the single process "Manage Records Creation" into its major subprocesses. In addition to its top and sublevel processes, the diagram also shows ICOMs. The model reflects the way classification is done in records management practices. The concepts embodied in the diagram enable records managers and IT personnel to perform their jobs efficiently and to comply with rules regarding the classification of records, an intrinsic element in the creation, maintenance, and disposal of records in an electronic environment or stored on electronic media.

The name of the highest level process is "Manage Current Records," as depicted in a context diagram in Fig. 5.2. The purpose of this process is to manage records created by a business or the government in a systematic manner, thereby preserving information appropriate to support its mission and business needs. The process of "Manage Current Records" reflects the fact that most people in the organizations engage in the first of three major activities involved in records management, namely creation. The two latter activities, namely maintenance and disposition, are carried out by a limited number of personnel, including records managers, who are assigned this responsibility. The maintenance and disposition of records are outside the viewpoint and scope of the model.

The three inputs that support the process of "Manage Current Records" are information, author, and action.

1. "Information" is analyzed data. It may consist of important or mundane data, or a combination of both. The value of information is determined from its contents. The content of the information should include its intention, evidence, purpose, story, course of action, or reasons to show what the information is about. Information may also have categories of security level. The explanation of risks and categories of information is defined by the National Institute of Standards and Technology (NIST). There are 12 categories of information with 3 levels of security: low, medium, and high as listed in Table 5.1.

   All three security levels may impact the organization depending on the damage done. The public disclosure or release of information that requires a low level of security may have a moderately serious impact on the organization, including a negative outcome or the potential to tarnish reputations, image, or functions, or requiring repairs to assets or resources. The unauthorized disclosure or release of information that requires a middle level of security may be "very" serious and severely impair an agency's mission, function, image, or reputation. It may also result in major damage, requiring extensive repairs to assets or resources.

Table 5.1 Categories of Information Level From High to Low

Level	Information Type
High	Investigation, intelligence-related, and security information
	Mission-critical information
	Life-critical information
Medium	Information about persons
	Financial, budgetary, commercial, and trade secret information
	Agency internal information
	Other federal agency information
	New technology or controlled scientific information
	Operational information
	System configuration management information
Low	Public information
	Other information

The unauthorized disclosure or release of information that requires a high level of security would cripple an organization completely and result in the loss of mission capability for an extended period. It is a catastrophic impact that would result in the loss of major assets or resources, and could be a threat to human life if related to medical information.

It is important to analyze and understand information in order to correctly determine the appropriate level of security required. The level of security can then be included in the "Description of Documents."

2. "Authors" are the creators of records. Authors are accountable to ensure that the information in records is correct, valid, and not fabricated. Details of authors, such as name, date of creation, or ID that can help to identify the author are important to record. It can help to establish that records that have been created are authentic.
3. "Action" is important for function-based classification and can help to determine how to classify the records. Function-based classification can capture the context in which information is created. The action of creating the information should be identified to describe the context of that information. Actions can have semantic relationships with other actions, and a collection of actions may relate to each other in many ways. These relationships become important, in the creation of classification schemes, when considering the distinction between functions and processes. For example, a plaintiff may file a case for divorce into the case file system. The action is divorce, but under Syariah law there are many types of divorce including fasakh, takhliq, khuluq, li'an, and talaq (Women's Center for Change, 2014). The word divorce on its own does

not identify which divorce the plaintiff would get. Therefore, action has a level of abstraction, and relates to other actions in the form of subtype, super type relationships. This form will break down the abstraction of actions to become more specific.

These inputs act as a source and result in the production of another set of information used to create, capture/save, and describe documents. There are two outputs:

1. "Create documents." Electronic documents contain indexing information known as metadata. Metadata is used to index and categorize the document, to allow for indexed storage, thereby allowing for easier and more precise retrieval of the document. The creation of electronic documents incorporates indexing and categorization along with other information such as the type of document, the date the document was created and filed, and other information depending on the exact document types and indexing requirements. Therefore, the "Create document" output consists of identifying and analyzing processes to produce a defined electronic document types and document groups, classification framework, and classification design.
2. "Capture/save documents." Electronic documents are captured or saved in a folder structure defined by the first output. In this process, documents are not only categorized for searching and retrieval purposes but also to accommodate the principles of records management for classification throughout the records life cycle. Documents (electronic and paper) can either be records or non-records, particularly in the United States. Documents are assigned as records, based on their value, use, and life cycle.

Mechanisms associated with the "Manage Current Records" process are essentially the resources that are required to complete the process of maintaining, controlling, and selecting records. It may include people with particular skills and tools such as IT physical facilities and infrastructure, people with particular skills including records managers, or any personnel who handles records in the organization.

The parenthesis markings at the arrow heads of controls and mechanisms in Fig. 5.2 indicate that these apply to lower levels on the model but are not shown on these diagrams to reduce clutter.

The controls or constraints for the model are represented in the form of guidelines, mandates and functions, laws and regulations (Franks, 2013; InterPARES2, 2008), de jure standards (Franks, 2013), and organizational structures (US Department of Defense, 2007). A de jure standard is a standard "concerning law" usually endorsed by a formal standards organization. The process for creating de jure standards is complex and rigid, requiring a stamp of approval and periodic audits. De jure standards like those created by IEEE and ISO are commonly referred to as consensus standards. These normally do not have any significant legal weight. True legal standards such as those created by Occupational Safety and Health Administration (OSHA) are different from consensus standards. In this model, de jure standards control the process of classification because government documents or records are official and in accordance with the law.

The outputs from context diagram (A-0) will be further explained in first, second and third level diagrams. The first level diagram (A0) describes two outputs from "Manage Current Records," which are "Create" and "Capture." The descriptions are made at basics levels explaining what are the outputs produced from "Create" and "Capture" processes. The processes occurring during "Create" are broken down into the second level (A1). The A1 describes processes involved in creating documents which include (1) make/receive, (2) gather requirements for defining documents, (3) create classification framework, and (4) classification design. On the other hand, the processes occur during "Capture" are explained in the third level (A2), which consists of three (1) capture, (2) save, and (3) assign records.

DECOMPOSED DIAGRAM FROM THE CONTEXT DIAGRAM (A-0): FIRST LEVEL

The lower levels of the model in diagram A-0 in Fig. 5.3 show the decomposed functions as specific processes. They reveal the processes involved in managing records after being created. Records creation subprocesses are broken down into "Create Documents" (A1) and "Capture/Save Documents" (A2).

The first level diagram (A-0) in Fig. 5.3 shows the "Manage Record Creation" process. It comprises two subprocesses, namely "Create Documents" and "Capture/Save Documents". Each subprocess' work is interrelated and occurs in sequential order. "Implementation guidelines" define how records are created.

Implementation guidelines are represented as the four controls described in context diagram A-0 (Fig. 5.2). They consist of guidelines describing the creator's mandates and functions; laws and regulations; standards (de jure); and organizational structure. All of these guidelines are important to be analyzed to form a records classification system.

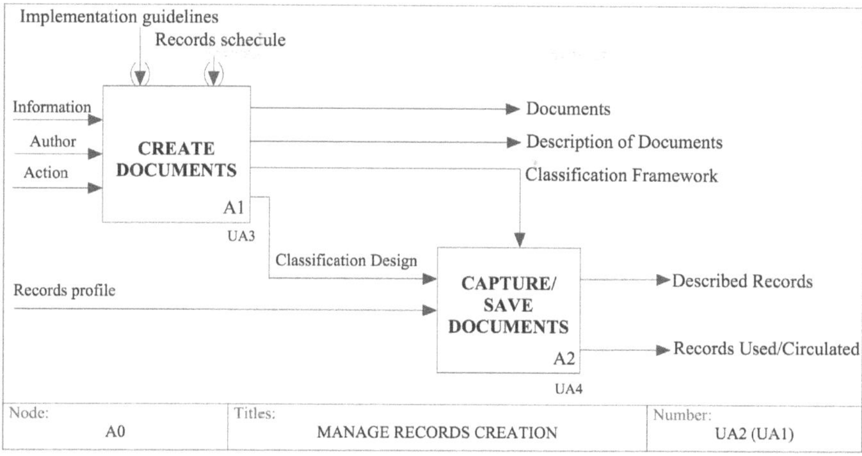

Figure 5.3 First level (A-0).

Documents are also assigned a records retention schedule to ensure they are kept for as long as required. Examples of legal records are bills of sale, business permits, claims and litigations, contracts, copyrights, correspondence-legal, deeds/titles, leases, licenses, mortgages, notes receivable, patents, stocks and bonds, and trademarks. All of these records, except leases (10 years), notes receivables (10 years), and trademarks (149 years), are to be kept permanently. The retention schedule for all records is determined by the National Archives of Malaysia.

Process 1: "Create Document"

The output from the "Create Documents" process is the creation of "Documents", "Description of Documents", "Classification Framework," and "Classification Design".

The first output is "Document". A document serves to establish one or several facts, and can be relied upon as proof thereof. In general, documents function as evidence of intentions, whereas records function as evidence of activities.

The second output is "Description of Documents", which contains a description of the document created, which is important as the evidence of activities to support business needs. The description consists of metadata. At this point, the metadata facilitates search and retrieval of documents.

The third output is "Classification Framework". A framework is defined as a real or conceptual structure intended to serve as a support or guide for building something that expands the structure into something useful (Rouse, 2005).

The "Classification Framework" provides the elements needed to construct a classification design. This is further explained in Fig. 5.5. The terms classification framework means that an IT developer should acknowledge that the classification of a record begins when it is created. The framework is a guideline to classify the document, and it becomes a control for the process "Capture/Save Documents".

The fourth output is "Classification Design". A design is a plan produced to show the look and function or workings of an object before it is built or made. This study focuses on records classification, which includes functions, actions, and processes as part of the design. The design of a records classification scheme should take into account the records life cycle, metadata, any litigation to which the organization was subjected, the structure of the organization, its business activities and processes, available technologies, and tools. The "Classification Design" will become an input for "Capture/Save Documents" process.

IT developers usually plan all the processes at the analysis phase. At this point, the processes such as creation of documents, classification, disposal, searching, and reporting should be defined in the analysis phase. Similarly, with records classification, the process should be identified as early as documents are created.

Process 2: "Capture/Save Documents"

The output from the "Capture/Save Documents" process is the capture of documents into a system used to manage them appropriately over time. The capture of documents as records requires the application of "descriptions of records" and "records profile" when the records are captured. This fixes the records within a business context and establishes management control. The timeframe of records availability is determined by the records retention schedule. "Descriptions of records" and "records profiles" provide information about who created and captured the records, when and for what business purpose, content, appearance, structure, and technical characteristics of the records.

The inputs for the "Capture/Save Documents" process are the "Records Profile" and "Classification Design." The "Records Profile" is captured to prepare records for transfer and might include any of the following elements (InterPARES2, 2008) such as archival or filing date; draft or version number; expression of the archival bond (via classification code, file identifier, record item identifier, dossier identifier); name of the author or creator; indication of or reference to copyright or other intellectual rights; name of the handling office; name of the office of primary responsibility; indication of any technical changes to the records; indication of any annotations; access restriction code; access privileges code; vital record code; planned disposition; indication of the record(s) transferred; name of the person effecting the transfer; name of the entity to whom the records are transferred; and date/time of the transfer.

The record profile consists of plans for the systematic generation of data entry forms designed to contain the attributes of records that attest to their identity and integrity, and which are generated when users create, send and/or, close records, are updated when users subsequently modify or annotate completed records, and remain inextricably linked to the records for the entire period of their existence while in the custody of the creator (InterPARES2, 2008).

All the extrinsic and intrinsic elements of records are incorporated to form the records profile. A key requirement for a records profile is to ensure that records are authentic, trustworthy, and reliable. Without these criteria, records may not be valid as evidence to protect an organization from risks that may damage its business function, mission, or reputation.

The example of a records profile from InterPARES1 shows both extrinsic and intrinsic elements. A "Record Profile" used to identify, authenticate, and contextualized information and the people, processes, and system that create, maintain, and use it. It allows users to control, manage, find, understand, and preserve information over time. A records profile is usually associated with the metadata of records. The elements that make up a records profile are depicted in Table 5.2 (InterPARES1, 2002).

The "Capture/Save Documents" process produces two outputs, namely the "Described Records" and "Records Circulated/Used."

Table 5.2 Records Profile Elements

Intrinsic Elements	Extrinsic Elements

• Presentation features:
  • Text, graphic, image, sound, layout, fonts, colors, hyperlinks, graphic attachment, sample rate of sound files, files resolution, and maps scale
• Electronic signature:
  • Electronic seal, authentication certificate of trusted third party, digital time-stamp, special sign
	• Name of author; name of originator; chronological date; name of place of origin of recordkeeping name of addressee(s); name of receiver (s); indication of action or matter; description of action or matter; name of writer; corroboration; attestation; and qualification of signature

The first output is "Described Records." "Described Records" is a process used to describe information so that people will know what it is about, understand their context and purpose, and can find easily whenever needed.

The second output is "Records Circulated/Used" where records are ready to be used and circulated. This process involves some form of transfer of the records for public or private use. Records that have been classified (from the "Capture/Save" process) are distributed for easy retrieval, effective management, and reliability. This process provides overall control and coordination of the transfer of completed records to the recordkeeping system.

DECOMPOSED DIAGRAM FOR RECORDS CLASSIFICATION MODEL: SECOND LEVEL

The second level describes the process of creating and classifying records. Fig. 5.4 depicts in detail each process that occurs in the "Create Documents" stage that results in the creation of a description of records, and consists of four subprocesses: "Make Documents" (A1), "Gather Requirements for Defining Documents" (A2), "Create Classification Framework" (A3), and "Design Classification" (A4).

Process 1: "Make/Receive Documents"

The process of "Make/Receive Documents" means that information is received from a system, but is not necessarily created in that system.

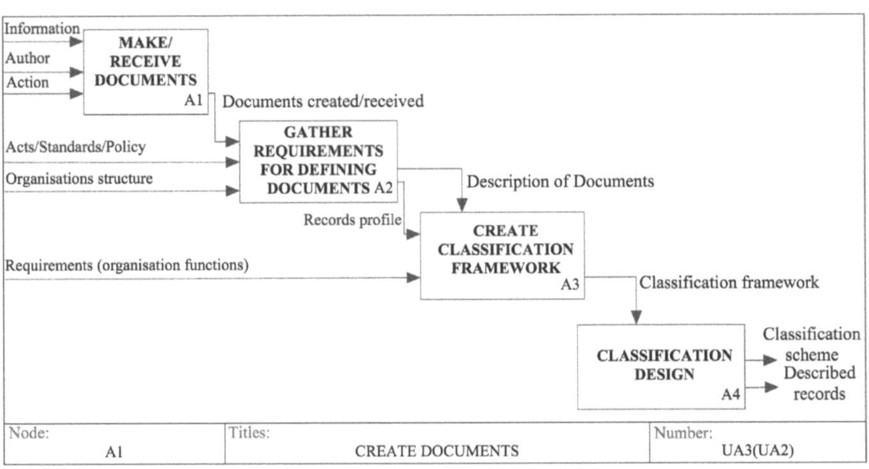

Figure 5.4 Second level (A1).

Documents may be regarded as received if they have gone through a digitizing process. The process "Make/Receive Documents" means that information is created from desktop applications, workflows, websites, databases, imaging system, or business system. The document is created electronically, together with its description of information, author, and action. At this point, the basic metadata for electronic documents are gathered. This basic metadata will be further expanded in the next process of "Gather Requirements for Defining Documents."

Process 2: "Gather Requirements for Defining Documents"

Requirements gathered to define electronic document types are obtained from a systematic analysis of an organization's business needs, legal and regulatory obligations, and broader community expectations, as well as an assessment of the organization's exposure to risk if these evidential requirements are not addressed. These requirements influence the type of records to be kept as evidence of business activity and how such records are to be maintained. Some requirements are stated explicitly in laws, regulations, and other instruments of authority, while others are implied by the environment in which the organization operates. The steps to gather the requirements are:

Step 1: Discovering the department's main activities to identify the functions of an organization and conduct a rigorous analysis of its business functions and activities. The idea is to extract a list of activities that the department carries out, later translated into document groups for each section of the department, e.g., judges' records and notebooks, lawyers' records, case records, cost assessments, and consultation records.

Step 2: Understanding the basic principles of classifying records. Based on functions, a class is referred to as a class of records. Five principles to guide classification (Orr, 2005; Schellenberg, 1956) are listed below:

1. Classes of records should be established only after records are created.
2. Each level in a classification should be consistent. ("Thus, if the primary classification is by functions, all headings at that level should be functions".)
3. Class titles should be chosen with care to reflect clearly the functions, activities, or transactions.
   a. Classes should be mutually exclusive.
   b. If titles are unclear or if classes are not mutually exclusive, scope notes (filing instructions) should be used. Separate classes should be created for facilitative/administrative and substantive or core business functions.

4. Important records related to policies, procedures, or classes should have separate classes, which should be broken down in subclasses. If this cannot be done, these records should be flagged.
5. Classifications schemes should be periodically reviewed and kept up to date.

Step 3: Defining record types for each record class (group)

1. Classification by function is based on the context of a record's creation and use, rather than on the content of the record itself. Thus, the record will be classified on the basis of why it exists.
2. The number of classification levels (usually three) required for classifying and titling records and other business information must be decided, as this will affect the depth of detail in the classification tool and the degree of training required by the users.
3. The terms used in the organization's business classification scheme form the basis for the terms used in the classification tool. These terms will need to be assessed for their suitability to be used as terms to support titling.

Step 4: Defining descriptions of documents for each record type

1. Defining descriptions of documents for searching and retrieval method
2. Defining descriptions of documents for the legal Syariah records
3. Using mandatory fields to define descriptions of documents
4. Specifying descriptions of documents field types

Step 5: Analyzing each part of the form to derive descriptions of documents

1. About author
2. About the case about the defendants/plaintiffs/witness list/attorney/judge
3. Describing the case and court minutes
4. Describing the cause
5. About the cost assessment
6. Description of order
7. Description of judgment

Records have categories such as vital, important, useful, and nonessential. The vital category has a catastrophic impact and the level of security is high. The impact to organizations lessens for categories important, useful, and nonessential. The example for this model is court records. There are four categories of Syariah cases such as "Mal," "Criminal," "Faraid," and "Appeal." Court records have eight types: indexes, orders, judgments, case files, witness lists, attorney records, and police records. Further explanation of each type is given in Table 5.3.

Table 5.3 Description of Court Records Types

Type	Description
Index	List of surnames litigants, plaintiffs, and defendants. Usually is brief and incomplete.
Court minutes	All actions of the courts are briefly recorded by the clerk in the minutes. The full range of court activities will fall within the recorded minutes.
Order	Orders of the courts are recorded by law in most jurisdictions for future reference.
Judgment	When the judgment is given by the court, the case is closed, but the clerk is required to make an extensive minute entry with abridgement of the case and its resolution in a special book of judgements.
Case file	Case files are among the valuable of all court records because they contain original copies of evidence, writs, testimony, subpoenas, and publications. Therefore, case files are considered complete. In these files will be found details that are not recorded in the minutes, orders, or judgments. Case files may contain one document or hundreds.
Witness list	Witness books and lists show the names of witness and the amounts received in payment.
Attorney record	Data concerning Syariah lawyer.
Police records	Police is called upon to perform some service such as official writs, summons, and subpoenas, and must execute all final judgments of the courts.

Step 6: Identify supporting records

It includes the documents such as letters, reports, notices, and applications (related).

The output of "Gather Requirements for Defining Documents" is "Descriptions of Documents." The documents are defined in "Create Documents" process.

Process 3: "Create Classification Framework"

The "Classification Framework" serves as the foundation for developing an actual system. The process of developing the framework requires input from standards, policies, and requirements (organizations and functional). These are the basic attributes that need to be identified at the early stage of development. Standards for managing records in Malaysia that may influence or should correspond with the development of records classification system include: standards produced by the National Archives, MS ISO 16,175-2 (2011), organizational procedures, and policies and guidelines provided by the government of Malaysia. All related standards, procedures, policies, and guidelines should be summarized and included in the framework in either narrative or graphical form. The scope of this requirement will depend on their relevance, suitability, and the needs of the organization. The functional requirements of systems should also be taken into consideration to ensure that they comply with standards for recordkeeping systems, such as MS ISO 16,175-2. The development of a classification framework must be aligned with an organization's needs, any relevant legislation, business, or functional needs. The failure to address any of these attributes correctly may affect to the development of the classification model.

Process 4: "Classification Design"

The "Classification Design" process is more detailed than the framework. Design is a process that combines sources from internal knowledge and analytical ability to produce a structured plan. "Classification Design" is made up of inputs from the records profile with reference to the "Classification Framework."

The "Classification Design" process consists of a relationship in which a thing or idea is linked or associated with something else, for example, the connections between function, activity, and process. A connection also describes the arrangement and relationship of actions that link one thing to another. The connection is presented in the form of a class and activity diagram to show a collection of functions and processes of classification. The diagram is a graphical representation of the workflow associated with activities and actions. Functions used to group related records are presented in the form of a class. For example, legal records are a class of records. The legal records class will decompose to legal records type, for example a case file or court minutes. Each case file will include various transactions such as publications, summons, or writs records. All of these processes will be presented in a class diagram, and be decomposed into an activity diagram to detail each process.

An example of "Classification Design" is by using a folder structure. It is created in a hierarchical structure, containing different levels of the organization's documents and records, and categorized based on the organization's functions. The folder structure is used as a document repository to store the organization's electronic documents and records. The folder must meet requirements of records functions and suit the organizational structure.

The outputs are the "Classification Scheme" and "Described Records."

DECOMPOSED DIAGRAM FOR RECORDS CLASSIFICATION MODEL: THIRD LEVEL

The "Capture/Save Documents" process is a guideline process to produce "Capture," "Save," "Describe Records," and "Assign Records." The flow, inputs, and outputs of the classification process are depicted in Fig. 5.5. This process is a unified approach that can cater for all types of record including accounting, corporate, personnel, insurance, legal, payroll, and taxation.

Process 1: "Capture"

This step is essential to manage records and capture them into a system that will appropriately manage and support their use over time. The capturing process includes the application of metadata as the documents are captured and establishing management control over them. Moreover, the process allows the documents to be retrieved, accessed, and managed over time.

Process 2: "Save"

The "Save" step is applicable for documents that are created from a system, instead of being received. The function of "save" is similar to "capture," as it allows the document to be managed, used, and maintained over time.

Process 3: "Assign Records"

In this process, documents and records are identified either as documents or records. The identification is referred from United States perspective as

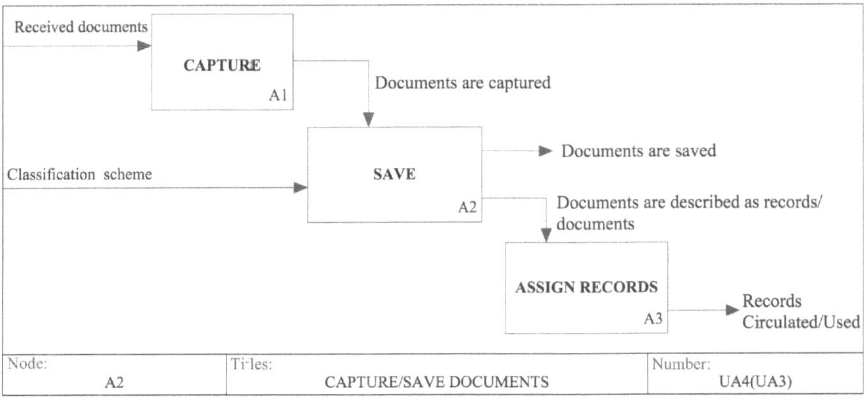

Figure 5.5 Third level (A2).

documents and records are different. Both documents and records are ready to be used and circulated.

SUMMARY OF RECORDS CLASSIFICATION MODEL

The proposed functional model is presented abstractly in the form of context diagram, and decomposed the processes into details in three levels of separate diagrams.

Fig. 5.6 is a summary of the RCM with the aim of facilitating an understanding in visualizing the complex process. It comprises the context diagram (A) decomposing the processes into three further levels in separate diagrams (B).

The RCM model adopts IDEF0 for developing the functional model. It consists of a node index, context diagram, and three levels of decomposed processes. The node index acts as a simple diagram to show the flow of the model. The context diagram is an abstraction of three levels showing processes with ICOMs.

Fig. 5.6 depicts the whole process involved in developing a functional model of records classification. It begins with a node index that acts as a road map to the flow of processes. The node index shows the processes and their outputs. The context diagram, labeled in box A, shows the management of records creation at the highest level. The diagram is simple however; it is

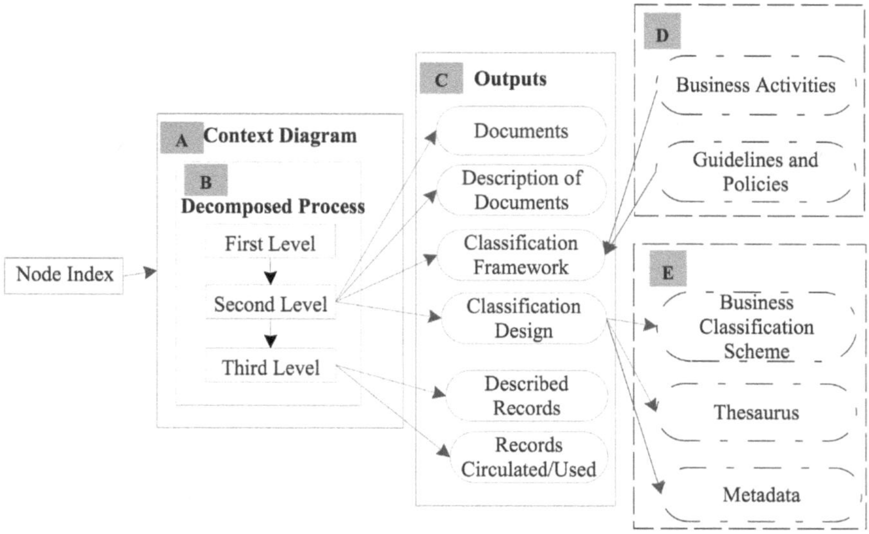

Figure 5.6 Summary of functional model—records classification model.

difficult to understand its function without decomposing their processes into different levels. Box B consists of three levels of processes, described in Figs. 5.3–5.5.

The first level describes in detail the content of the context diagram. It depicts both processes involved, namely the creation of documents and capture/save of documents. The creation and capture/save documents steps are further broken down into second and third levels.

The second level depicts the process for creating documents. Once the document is created or received, all details such as information about its author, actions involved in creating the document, contents, structure, and context are composed into descriptions of documents. A document produced is not only about its contents, but comes together with its descriptions. The descriptions of documents are presented in a structured form, normally known as metadata. All information such as inputs, constraints, and mechanisms needed while creating a document will be gathered to form a classification framework and design.

The third level shows simpler processes involved in the capture/save documents. The classification occurs at the beginning of documents creation. The documents retrieved are captured, while the documents created are saved. Both have similar function, which is to save the document into the system. Then, the documents are assigned and described as either document or records, and then distributed or used. The classification of documents allows documents that have been received or captured and identified as records to be assigned classification codes from the classification scheme; for these codes to be added with the identifying metadata; for registration numbers to be assigned to documents based on the registration scheme; and for these numbers to be added to the identifying metadata. All of the outputs from the second and third levels are depicted in box B.

The RCM explains all the processes involved, as pictured in boxes A, B, and C. Although boxes C and D are not explained, they relate to the processes included in those three boxes. Box D shows the arrows from D to C, addressing the business activities and sets of guidelines and procedures are the inputs of classification framework. The existing sources of guidelines and procedures are US DoD 5015.2–0, MoReqs, NOARK, UK National Archives Requirements, National Archives of Australia's Specifications, and New Zealand's System Standard. On the other hand, box E shows arrows out from C to E. The classification design should include all elements from the classification framework and design the flow of classification to provide for the business classification scheme, thesaurus, and metadata.

A classification scheme is established from an analysis of business activities (included in classification framework), based on RM principles. The classification process establishes that a document has been selected for incorporation into the records of the creator and places it in relation to the business process of which it is a part of, and action that generated it. It may also relate to the administrative structure where the record is created. The classification scheme results in the creation of aggregations of records in series and classes of records that may be subject to further processes. These processes and matters are usually identified through new metadata such as classification codes, registration numbers, and inherited metadata, as well as the name of the creator, any copyright or intellectual rights, and the name of the primary responsible office, any access restrictions, access privileges, any vital record code, and any planned disposition.

CHARACTERISTICS OF ELECTRONIC RECORDS SYSTEM

Information technology system or information system is defined as the infrastructure, processes, and technology used to store, generate, manipulate, and transmit information to support an organization (ARMA-Glossary). The system is a bridge study from business and computer science using the theoretical foundations of information and computation. Information system typically includes an ICT component but is not purely concerned with ICT, focusing instead on the end use of IT. Information system helps to control the performance of business process, which generally focuses upon processing information within organizations, business enterprises, and society (O'Brien, 2003).

On the other hand, electronic records management system concerns more with how system should capture, receive, and preserve records according to their characteristics. This is to maintain records authenticity, reliability, integrity, trustworthiness, and usability throughout lifecycle. Hence, electronic records system is a system specifically designed to manage the maintenance and disposition of records throughout its lifecycle. The system maintains the content, context, structure, and links between records to enable their accessibility and support values as evidence. Electronic records system requires partnership with information technology and records management fields to support requirements to access records and controls that handle records. Such requirements are as follows (RIM International, 2009):

1. Access criteria:
   a. policies stipulating who has access records and on restricted records,
   b. assurance that access and retrieval are timely,

  c. assurance that records are retrievable by authorized users only,
  d. relevant metadata applicable to the captured record is maintained for the lifecycle of the record or until otherwise designated, and
  e. recognition on privacy issues.
2. Controls on records:
  a. measures to monitor who has access to records,
  b. safeguard the records from unauthorized access to ensure that the integrity of the records is maintained at all times,
  c. audit trail of all records to capture all activity to ensure the records are not compromised,
  d. demonstration that migration, system malfunctions, upgrades, and regular maintenance of records systems will not infringe upon the integrity of the records
  e. methodologies to protect the confidentiality, privacy, and security of records from unauthorized access, tampering, or disposal,
  f. validation/verification techniques that ensure system and functional compliance requirements are met,
  g. records protection and preservation requirements also must be met,
  h. ability of the records system to preserve records and their associated metadata and be accessible throughout its retention period, and
  i. ability of the records system to preserve the records and metadata selected for long-term or archival storage, and ensure these records and metadata remain accessible in the future.

However, most of the systems in organizations are business system (some called as information system) including e-Syariah system. The business system serves as an automated system that creates or manages data about organization's activities. This includes application whose primary purpose is to facilitate transactions between an organizational unit and its customers such as e-commerce system, customized database, and finance and human resources systems. Typically, this system contains dynamic data that is commonly subjected to constant updates (timely), can be transformed (manipulatable), and holds current data (nonredundant).

Many of organizations implement business system for managing electronic records by partly taking records management requirement into consideration (Oberg & Borglund, 2006). For example, Iacovino (2004) describes Australian national electronic health records system does not follow the records management requirements such as reliability and authenticity. The similar situation happens in e-Syariah system by only taking into consideration the technical aspects and neglecting the records management requirements. Neither developed nor developing countries could ensure the complete utilization of records management requirements into the electronic system (whether records or business systems).

Records management requirement should be captured at the creation level to be able to maintain through preservation. It takes a proactive approach to design and develop electronic records system. This approach has to be supported by standards and regulations, e.g., MoReqs (2002), ISO 15,489 (2001), DoD 5152 (2007), and Acts. It is also crucial to identify characteristics of the electronic records system such as authenticity, reliability, integrity, and usability. These characteristics are maintained by the following attributes:

1. creating records in context,
2. managing and maintaining records,
3. maintaining records for as long as required,
4. records management metadata can be configured,
5. records can be reassigned, reclassified, closed, duplicated, and extracted,
6. reports can be undertaken, and
7. security processes in place.

Besides these characteristics, the core element or functional requirements of electronic records system should also be identified. The functional requirements include the processes for creation, maintenance, dissemination, administration, making multimedia repository, enterprise content management, and collaboration. Classification, along with capture and identification, is included in creation level. Electronic records are captured, identified, and classified uniquely to ensure the content, structure, and context of creation are fixed in time and space (e-SPARK, 2008).

Documents, the inputs from desktop applications, workflows, websites, databases, systems, applications, and emails are captured with metadata through capturing process. The process involves aggregation to from files into classes. Aggregation takes place before records are classified. The process accumulates related electronic records entities that when combined may exist above the level of single electronic record objects, for example a file. Aggregation represents the relationships that exist between related electronic records and the system or environment in which they were created, and are recorded in their metadata links. These aggregations are typically controlled within a classification scheme in an electronic records management system (e-SPARK, 2008).

In electronic records management system, information is managed as records objects and then aggregates these objects into a set of series or files. At this point, organizations should take into account their business needs when determining suitable records aggregation (such as by function, activity, or transaction). Within a classification scheme, records' contextual characteristics are attributed through a structure based on business processes. An analysis of the unique business functions and activities of an organization independent of organization's administrative structure produce a functional classification scheme. Functional classification scheme is believed to be more flexible and stable because business units and structures are likely to change over time.

Standard procedures of new information systems are designed and developed to perform an analysis of the business activities and to capture requirements from businesses, legal aspects, users, customers, and others involved (Oberg & Borglund, 2006). This is to define and make information intelligible, and the process is known as formalization of information. This is crucial for managing information in business system by determining the types of information, properties, and interrelationship involved (Shipman & McCall, 1994, 1999). In other words, this is the process to identify and determine the extrinsically and intrinsically records forms.

Records, whether virtual or physical, have content, context, structure, and process (Bearman, 1994; McKemmish, Piggott, Reed, & Upward, 2005; Thomassen, 2001). However, these features do not make records unique in relation to other information. Records have criteria to make them unique and different from other information, such as evidence of actions and transactions, accountability, which is tightly connected to evidence, relation to processes, and preservation, short term, long term, or permanent (Schellenberg, 1956; Thomassen, 2001).

CONCLUSION

Although lawyers know better about legal records and legislation procedures, they are rarely good records managers. IT people are also not good record managers. During the development of electronic systems to manage legal records, it is important to ensure that responsible personnel lead the development of the system. Law firms in Malaysia continue to use both paper and electronic records keeping systems. These systems are usually organized in a client-matter-folder hierarchical system, where each client is assigned a unique number based on the client matter. The manual system is used to manage the official records of clients, and electronic systems are used by lawyers to manage their own work-in-progress.

Law firms also use document type naming conventions where documents are filed by the type of documents (letter, memo, fax, agreement, etc.).

Records classification has gained a reputation in the records management field since its introduction by Schellenberg in the early 1950s. Many organizations have moved from subject-based classification to records classification because of the benefits it offers to the organizations. Records classification uses the FAT model approach as a reference. This approach is widely used and acknowledged especially in prominent classification projects such as DIRKS (2006a, 2006b, 2006c, 2006d) and Library and Archives Canada. (2006b). However, due to practical limitations in adoption, the FAT model approach has led to slight deviations in use of the terminology, resulting in the use of the terms function, activity, and transaction for DIRKS and function, sub-function, and activity for BASCS. Alberts et al. (2010) suggest that instead of using the FAT terminology, organizations should use a goal-state-action approach in which function is equal to goal and end state, while activities are equal to action. The suggested approach is more easy to understand and explicit. In making the goal-state-action approach workable, one must define functions and processes, which are the results of the relationship between actions and processes. An action is defined as a description of an act, while a process is a sequence or flow of actions. Single actions cannot address the flow of information. Therefore, a function is important to be identified in a record because it provides for the flow of information and actions.

Therefore, a framework or model with structures and elements clearly labeled for developing a classification scheme is helpful as users prefer it (Orr, 2005). Correct techniques are required to list functions hierarchically. However, in reality, structures or elements may be unclear thereby creating an artificial and logical model which, it could be claimed, is a representation of the real world. Problems may arise if organization structure is attached to a classification group because it could become meaningless if the organization is restructured or if staff switches the departments. To overcome this problem, a dynamic classification system can attach metadata to records to place them into virtual categories for the purpose of aiding retrieval function (Orr, 2005).

CHAPTER SIX

Conclusion

INTRODUCTION

The authors have attempted to examine the existence of classification for managing electronic records at public agencies in Malaysia. The data gathered for writing the book was first obtained through conducting a case study at the Department of Judiciary, Malaysia, which serves as a snapshot study. It was a requirement to carry out the snapshot study as the information gathered is useful for proposing a functional model to be used by the public agencies of the country. Although the snapshot study focused on legal records, the model proposed can be applied to other organization as it is generic in nature.

Upon analyzing existing models on classification and records management, it was evident that no classification model was used or referred to for managing records in public agencies in Malaysia. This became the motivation to create a model to be used by the public agencies if Malaysia wishes to be at par with other developed countries in the case of electronic records. The model was proposed using functional modeling approach which consists of three components typical for any model. These are input, process, and output. Upon closely following the suggested approach by FIPS 1993, the model was successfully constructed and then validated. This new model comprises node index, context diagram, and decomposed diagrams, as discussed in Chapter 5.

The current practice in classification system is of adopting and considering the IT requirements as the system was designed by IT team who has no background of records management. Thus, neither subject-based nor function-based classification was adopted in creating the system. The e-Syariah system, particularly the Syariah Court Case Management System module, does not cover the entire phases in life cycle of records namely the creation (capture, identify, classify), maintenance (access, security, retention, disposition), dissemination (search, retrieve, render), transfer (acquisition, arrangement), and preservation. Instead, the system provides a case and workflow management structure that integrates the processes related to management

Records Classification: Concepts, Principles and Methods
ISBN 978-0-08-102238-2
http://dx.doi.org/10.1016/B978-0-08-102238-2.00006-8

of cases for 102 Syariah courts nationwide that merely covered for documents creation and dissemination. The system was developed entirely based on the technical (the IT) point of view and perspective by referring to one of the software development life cycle (SDLC) which is the planning, analysis, design, implementation, and maintenance. The SDLC method is referred to for the purpose of guiding the system developers (the technical team) at each system development phase, starting from planning to until the system is ready to deploy. On the other hand, the records life cycle is referred to as the stages of records life span, which act as one of the inputs/requirements to the system development. Since the finding indicates that records life cycle has not been taken into consideration, therefore, not all phases in the records life cycle are adopted. This confirms that classification, appraisal, and preservation were not included as phases in the Syariah Court Case Management System.

Although the system created is sufficient and appropriate for search and retrieve functions, it has ignored the complete records life cycle concept where classification is also a part of it. Searching can be done using metadata such as date, name, subject, or keywords. The first sub-objective has been successfully achieved which is to assess the current classification system in Malaysia by means of interviews at Department of Syariah Judiciary, Malaysia and National Archives of Malaysia. Since there are no records classification systems being implemented in public sector organizations, the proposed model can serve as a basis to develop such a system in organizations in Malaysia.

Analyses of the 20 models (divided into two categories: functional and conceptual) also discovered that there is no single model specifying records classification presented in functional form.

This book has contributed to both theory and practice of classification in specific and records management in general. The theoretical contribution has apparently enriched the body of knowledge of records management field for the following reasons:

1. Literature in the area of classification is scarce. The lack of research on classification has also led to a situation where classification is being regarded similar in all information-related fields. Thus, classification practiced in the library and information science had been attempted to be applied to records management. However, the principles of classification from both fields are different in application. The minimally explored research has contributed to the fact that classification from the records management perspective is further understudied despite it is the core element in records management. Since the proposed classification

model is based on functions, the context of records can be preserved by identifying the relation of records functions with its actions, authors, and constraints that control the creation process. This is crucial to ensure records *fonds* are secured and intact in time and space. The impaired *fonds* contribute to inauthentic and untrustworthy records.

2. A model for electronic records classification based on function is not widely explored. In addition to comprising all the records management principles, the proposed model also focuses on the crucial issue in electronic records management, i.e., the creation of reliable records and preservation of the authenticity over time.
3. The current records classification models are complicated, lengthy, and generic in nature covering all the phases in the records life cycle. On the contrary, the new proposed model is more focused on the process of classifying classification, i.e., more methodical and practical in manner, which seem to be in line and fits the requirement for digital recordkeeping system.

With such a distinct characteristic, the new records classification model thus has significantly contributed to the theory or the body of knowledge in records management field.

The practical contribution of the book is also remarkable whereby:

1. Organizations can adopt the model for creating their own classification system. The information-related policy makers at large and records classification in specific can benefit since most organizations are not practicing records classification as the result of not knowing how to go about creating the system in addition to not having records management policy. Thus, the model can be a starting point for developing records classification system in Malaysia.
2. The effectiveness of management is referred to the capability of government in providing good performance (An, Shuyang, & Wei, 2011). Currently, this is achieved by IT professional by providing the state-of-the-art technology for converting a manual management system to an automatic one. On the other hand, the efficiency of organizations can be gained if business is conducted the right way by minimizing time, cost, and effort with maximum results. This can be achieved through records classification, as records are assets that provide power to organizations (Foscarini, 2009).
3. Classification can also guarantee the continuity of business by ensuring vital records are kept safely (An et al., 2011) to prevent the organization from collapsing. With classification, all records (vital, useful, important, and non-useful) are categorized to determine their values and functions.

Classification system is best drawn alongside with policies, procedures, standards, best practices, and complies with legislations. The authors have successfully developed a records classification functional model which takes into consideration all the elements complying with the records management principle.

4. The proposed model is generic and simple in nature, with easy language to understand, simple explanation for each process, and explicit functional model for the early classification preparation process. It is evident from the panel of expert's approval that the proposed model can be used for basic guidance because all the processes in relation to classification are identified and the logical sequence of process order is also appropriate.
5. The Malaysian government would also be able to create and increase awareness about the importance of managing electronic records and implementing records classification. It is proven in the developed countries that records management has helped the nation in many aspects particularly in relation to increasing the productivity, seen as practicing democracy, accountability, and transparency (Mnjama & Wamukoya, 2007; Wamukoya & Mutula, 2005). This will eventually promote the importance of classifying records which finally resulted in improved service delivery.

There were obstacles in writing this book. First, there was a lack of an effective benchmark. Reference sources for records classification model are scarce, which contributed to the lack of an effective benchmark. This is partly due to the fact that classification, in particular, is an under-researched area and records management, in general, is an underexplored area of study compared to library and information science.

Also, records classification system is a cross-discipline area, where both theory and practice are important to make the system work in the real world. Since these authors focus and propose the model from the records management perspective, the aspect of classification in IT does not receive equal attention. This is evident from the professional feedbacks indicating that they are skeptical to implement the model because it is linear in process, whereas the current practice employs records continuum even though the model is appropriate and relevant.

In addition, the limited nature of information was reported by the personnel in charge of records classification in the case study, and it is reasonable therefore to infer that the answers to the interview tend to reflect the rather limited perception of classification in both theory and practice among the interviewees. This is because the interviewees are not trained in records management. They are only trained in IT.

Another limitation is that the case study was confined only to one sector (legal). The selection of only one sector is sufficed for the purpose of this study, but it should be extended to more sectors in the future. This is to provide more holistic view and identify rigorous components of records classification in Malaysian perspective.

The authors have also experienced the absence of an existing benchmark against which to compare the results of the interviews. Despite the limitations, this book is valuable in the way it has developed and refined a method specifically for records classification research in public agencies, and the interview successfully explored issues which were developed with this objective in mind.

As mentioned earlier, classification received less attention compared to appraisal, preservation, terminologies, concepts, and generic guidelines. The concept does not receive priority as there is no enforcement for applying the endeavor for electronic records. Although there was a circular in 2007 regarding classifying paper records, but it was without any enforcement. Moreover, the National Information Technology Agenda (NITA) (1996) has embraced the concept of utilizing ICT with the aim to set up a knowledge-based society and economy by the year 2020, without addressing the need of records management or the importance of managing information. The failure to address records management requirements and the imbalanced attention between ICT and information led to a lack of awareness among civil servants about the importance of records management in general and classification in particular. Also, there is a potential risk that digital records would not be captured and protected systematically (Lowry & Thurston, 2012).

The evidence of imbalanced focus between ICT and information can be observed from Malaysian ranking as an e-government leader, which dropped to 32nd spot in 2010, then further declined to the 40th spot in 2012 (United Nations, 2012). The focus on technological aspect alone as a core element in the e-government initiative (Zouridis & Thaens, 2003) has resulted in a total and partial failure (35% and 50%, respectively) in implementing the project (Heeks, 2003). Potential impediments of the failure were attributed by the imbalanced attention given to technology and information (Nawi, Rahman, & Ibrahim, 2005; Ramli, 2012). Hence, in realizing the knowledge-based society, the information embedded in records should be given equal attention and acknowledged as strategic equal and at par to technology, since both are central to the success of the nation.

Apparently, records management is central to the organizational success, competency and continuity (An, 2009; Mnjama & Wamukoya, 2007; Shafie, 2007). Records management could differentiate a successful organization from organization that fails. Thus, this study could spark a more serious attention and effort into electronic records management initiatives. A complete and holistic infrastructure should be in place inclusive of the technology; laws, regulations, and standards; framework, policy, and training; and budget, which also act as an audit list for managing electronic records (Ismail & Jamaludin. 2009). This book could serve as an eye opener to the policy maker to always give high priority to electronic records management.

Electronic records are managed as national assets, resources, and trusted information in the e-government strategy (An, 2009). Hence, the electronic records can become a competitive advantage for organization (Chosky, 2006). In the United States, New Zealand, and the UK, the electronic records management is embedded into the e-government strategy. However, literature on electronic records management in e-government strategy is still little even though electronic records management is vital to effective e-government strategy for seamless services to public. Moreover, good electronic records management strengthens e-government strategy by supporting business continuity, security and risk management, legal compliance and accountability, evidence-based decision making and transparency, good governance and public trust, good performance, and government capability building. Thus, there is a need of investment between government authorities and records management professionals across domains and time dimension for ensuring electronic records are well managed according to legal and regulatory systems and records management principles.

President Barack Obama signed the Presidential Memorandum for Managing Government Records on November 28, 2011, which marked the beginning of an executive branch-wide effort to reform records management policies and practices and to develop a 21st century framework for the management of government records (Memorandum for the Heads of Executive Departments and Agencies and Independent 2012). This shows that records management play major roles in determining the security, efficiency and integrity of the country beginning with managing the government information embedded in records. Thus, this study could warrant the implementation of records management initiative nationwide. The government should enforce its implementation supported by appropriate laws and regulations. Only with records management in place, the government can be seen as practicing democracy with a degree of transparency and accountability in serving its citizens. Without records management, not only records are exposed to risks but they may also fall into the hands of the unauthorized parties such as intelligence and espionage, and thus jeopardize and endanger the sovereignty of the nation.

Malaysia is also striving toward establishing a knowledge-based economy and knowledge society where information is central to all activities. A complete or holistic records management practice inclusive of classification enables the country to be more productive, efficient, effective, and competent. Function-based classification is a suitable approach that manages records in context, especially for the highly anticipated "Big Data" phenomena worldwide including Malaysia (Computing Community Consortium, 2012).

Theoretically, the electronic records classification should be prepared before developing the system or creating the records. This theory of classification is well accepted in many countries such as the United States, Europe, and Australia. In Malaysia, the process of classification is done in reversed order. The dynamic documentation management system (DDMS) project was developed to increase search and retrieval, and protect the institutional memory (Shafie, 2014). Upon completion of the DDMS project, the Malaysian government realized the need for a classification system, and put the implementation of the DDMS on hold. This would not have happened if the classification was well embraced from the beginning.

Thus, the Malaysian government should enforce the implementation of effective records management in all public agencies in parallel with e-government initiative and increase the level of IT literacy in order to establish knowledge society. This can be facilitated by better awareness, understanding, and acceptance of records management.

It is time for the government of Malaysia to give balanced attention to information and technology. Giving imbalanced attention would jeopardize information which is the life blood of the nation. "I" (information) is equally important as "T" (technology), and leaving information behind might invite catastrophes. This could be achieved by developing a holistic information policy in Malaysia to avoid the loss or leakage of information.

With the government of Malaysia insisting that public agencies be innovative, the application of records classification in specific, and records management initiative in general, should be seen as a part of that innovative process. In this regard, the adequate information delivered to the right place at the right time for decision making, particularly when an agency is delivering its service or adjusting strategy, is essential; records management could provide answer to this. Records management is a corporate requirement which serve as a basis for good practice and governance, and is also an essential element in reducing the risk of increased liability and decreased opportunity that accompany poor records management practice.

Through Vision 2020, Malaysia has developed a positive vision in which information and related services have the potential to promote steady and sustainable growth to increase global competitiveness, to open up job opportunities, and to improve the quality of life of its people. Malaysian organizations are also encouraged to meet the International ISO 9000 series of standards. The first requirement is that they must demonstrate and practice good information management. Thus, organizations should recognize that records management can make a significant difference in their ability to comply with the requirements of the standards, and enable them to fulfill the goal of Vision 2020. Records management in general and classification in particular has many untold advantages for the country.

REFERENCES

Ab.Aziz., M. J. (2004). Implementation of an electronic document management system based on network protocols. *Jurnal Teknologi Maklumat dan Multimedia*, 27–34.

Abraxas. (2013). *Abraxas records resources report: Paper vs. electronic files*. Retrieved from http://abraxasworldwide.com/wp-content/themes/Abraxas/kd-pdf.php?id=867.

Abrera, J. B. (1974). Traditional classification: Characteristics, uses and problems. *Drexel Library Quarterly*, *10*(4), 21–36.

Alberts, I., Schellinck, J., Eby, C., & Marleau, Y. (2010). Bridging functions and processes for records management. *Canadian Journal of Information and Library Science*, *34*(4), 365–390.

An, X. (May 30–31, 2009). The electronic records management in e-government strategy: Case studies and the implications. In *International conference on networking and digital society, ICNDS'09, Guiyang* (Vol. 1) (pp. 17–20). Retrieved from http://ieeexplore.ieee.org/xpls/abs_all.jsp?arnumber=5116201&tag=1.

An, X., Shuyang, S., & Wei, Z. (2011). Managing electronic records in e-government: Current trends and future directions internationally. In *International conference on management and service science (MASS)*. Retrieved from http://ieeexplore.ieee.org/xpls/abs_all.jsp?arnumber=5999074.

ANSI/NISO Z39.50. (2003). *Information retrieval: Application service definition and protocol specification*. Bethesda: National Information Standards Organisation.

Archives New Zealand. (2010). Digital Record keeping Standard. Section 27 *Issued under the Public Records Act, 2005*. Retrieved from http://archives.govt.nz/sites/default/files/S5_Digital_Recordkeeping_Standard.pdf.

Ariff, M. (2008). *Data classification: Why it is important and how to do it*. Retrieved from *http://www.computerweekly.com/feature/Data-classification-why-it-is-importa nt-and-how-to-do-it.*

Bantin, P. C. (2001). The Indiana University Electronic Records Project: Lessons Learned. *The Information Management Journal*, *35*(1), 16–25.

Bantin, P. (2002). *Electronic records management: A review of the work of a decade and a reflection of future directions*. New York: Marcel.

Bates, M. J. (1999). The invisible substrate of information science. *Journal of the American Society for Information Science*, *50*, 1043–1050.

Batley, S. (2007). The 'I' in information architecture: The challenge of content management. *Aslib Proceedings: New Information Perspectives*, *59*(2), 139–151.

Bearman, D. (1994). *Electronic evidence: strategies for managing records in contemporary organizations*. Pittsburgh: Archives and Museum Informatics.

Bearman, D. (2006). Moments of risk: Identifying threats to electronic records. *Archivaria*, *62*, 15–46.

Bearman, D. (November 6, 2007). *Fundamental issues for electronic records management. Seminar on electronic documents: Management and preservation*. Belo Horizonte, Brazil: Archives and Museum Informatics. Retrieved from http://www.archimuse.com/papers/200711-bearman-brazil/200711-bearman-brazil.html.

Bedford, D., & Morelli, J. (2006). Introducing information management into the workplace: A case study in the implementation of business classification file plans from the Sector Skills Development Agency. *Records Management Journal*, *16*(3), 169–175.

Berg, H. F. (2009). *Noark: The Norwegian Records Management Standard*. Retrieved from http://www.nacr.cz/dlm/presentations/berg.pdf.

Borko, H. (1968). Information science: What is it? *American Documentation*, *19*(1), 3–5.

Botsch, R. E. (2011). *APLS 301 scope and research methods in political science: Concepts, variables, and measurement*. Retrieved from http://www.usca.edu/polisci/apls301/Text/Chapter%204.%20Concepts,%20Variables,%20and%20Measurement.htm.

Bowker, G. C., & Star, S. L. (1999). *Sorting things out: Classification and its consequences.* Cambridge, Mass: The MIT Press.
Bowker, G. C., & Star, S. L. (2000). Invisible mediators of action: Classification and the ubiquity of standards. *Mind, Culture, and Activity*, 7(1–2), 147.
Broughton, V. (2010). Bliss Bibliographic Classification (2nd ed.). In *Encyclopedia of library and information science*, Vol. 1(1) (pp. 650–659). Abingdon: Taylor & Francis.
Broughton, V., & Mills, J. (2011). *Bliss bibliographic classification* (2nd ed.). Munich: De Gruyter Saur.
Buckland, M. K. (1991). Information as thing. *Journal of the American Society for Information Science*, *42*(5), 351–360.
Budd, J. M. (1995). An epistemological foundation for library and information science. *Library Quarterly*, *65*(3), 295–318.
Budd, J. M. (2011). Meaning, truth, and information: Prolegomena to a theory. *Journal of Documentation*, *67*(1), 6–74.
Burge, S. (2011). *The systems engineering toolbox. Draft version for comment.* Retrieved from http://www.burgehugheswalsh.co.uk/uploaded/documents/FM-Tool-Box-V1.0.pdf.
Business Dictionary. (n.d.). *Model.* Retrieved from http://www.businessdictionary.com/definition/model.html.
Campbell, E. G. (1941). Functional classification of archival material. *The Library Quarterly*, *11*(4), 431–441.
Capurro, R., & Hjørland, B. (2003). The concept of information. *Annual Review of Information Science and Technology*, *37*(1), 343–411.
Carleton College. (2009). *What is a model.* Retrieved from http://serc.carleton.edu/introgeo/models/WhatIsAModel.html.
Carter, M. C. (1998). *The methodology of arrangement: A case study of the Department of the Provincial Secretary of British Columbia* (Master thesis). University of British Columbia.
Chaffey, D., & Wood, S. (2005). *Business information management – Improving performance using information systems.* Harlow: Prentice Hall.
Charman, D. (1984). *Records surveys and schedules: A RAMP study with guidelines.* Paris: UNESCO.
Chinyemba, A., & Ngulube, P. (2005). Managing records at higher education institutions: A case study of the University of KwaZulu-Natal, Pietermaritzburg Campus. *South African Journal of Information Management*, 7(1), 1–19. Retrieved from http://general.rau.ac.za/infosci/raujournal/default.asp?to=peervol7nr1.
Chosky, C. E. B. (2006). *Domesticating information: Managing documents inside the organization.* London: The Scarecrow Press.
Computing Community Consortium (CCC). (2012). *Challenges and opportunities with big data.* Retrieved from http://www.cra.org/ccc/files/docs/init/bigdatawhitepaper.pdf.
Cook, T. (1992). Mind over matter: Towards a new theory of archival appraisal. In B. L. Craig (Ed.), *The archival imagination: Essays in honour of Hugh A. Taylor* (pp. 38–70). Ottawa: ACA.
Cook, T. (1997). What is past is prologue: A history of archival ideas since 1898, and the future paradigm shift. *Archivaria*, *43*(1), 17–63.
Cook, T. (2001). Archival science and postmodernism: New formulations for old concept. *Archival Science*, *1*(1), 3–24.
Cook, T. (2007). Electronic records, paper minds: The revolution in information management and archives in the post-custodial and post-modernist era. *Archives & Social Studies: A Journal of Interdisciplinary Research*, *1*, 399–443.
Council, G. (2015). *Should machines do the work or humans.* Retrieved from http://www.parascript.com/blog/machines-or-humans-do-the-work/.
Cox, R. J., & Duff, W. (1997). *Archives and Museum Informatics*, *11*, 223. http://dx.doi.org/10.1023/A:1009008706990.
Creswell, J. W. (2009). *Research design: Qualitative, quantitative, and mixed methods approaches.* Los Angeles: Sage.

Cunningham, A. (2008). *Going Global: Developing globally harmonised software specifications for records, National Archives of Australia, Staff Paper.* Retrieved from http://www.naa.gov.au/about- us/partnerships/conferences/asa.aspx.

Davenport, T. H., & Prusak, L. (2000). *Working knowledge: How organizations manage what they know.* Boston: Harvard Business School Press.

Department of Defense (DoD). (2003). *Records management function and information.* Retrieved from http://www.archives.gov/era/pdf/rmsc-19951006-dod-rm-function-and-information-models.pdf.

DeMarco, T. (1979). *Structured analysis and system specification. Englewood-Cliffs.* NJ: Yourdon Press.

Dissertation-help.co. (1999). *From simple to broader to a more in-detailed theoretical framework definition that will sort out each & every confusion in your head.* Retrieved from http://www.dissertation-help.co.uk/dissertation_guide/Define-theoretical-framework.htm.

Duff, W. (1996). Ensuring the preservation of reliable evidence: A research project funded by the NHPRC. *Archivaria, 42,* 28–45.

Duranti, L. (1998). *Diplomatics. New uses for an old science.* Lanham: Scarecrow Press.

Duranti, L. (2007). *System of record definition.* Retrieved from http://forums.rmaa.com.au/showthread.php?t=799.

Duranti, L., & MacNeil, M. (Spring 1997). The preservation of the integrity of electronic records: An overview of the UBC-MAS research project. *Archivaria, 42,* 46–67.

Eastwood, T. (March 16, 2007). The theory and practice of description in the digital era. In *Paper delivered at the second meeting on archival information databases, sponsored by the Brazilian Society of Archivists, Rio de Janeiro.*

Eaton, J. J., & Bawden, D. (1991). What kind of resource is information? *International Journal of Information Management, 11*(2), 156–165.

Erden, M. S., Komoto, H., Van Beek, T. J., D'Amelio, D., Echavarria, E., & Tomiyama, T. (2008). A review of function modelling: Approaches and applications. *Artificial Intelligence for Engineering Design, Analysis and Manufacturing, 22,* 147–169.

Evans, M. J. (2007). Archives of the people, by the people, for the people. *American Archivist, 70*(2), 387–400.

Federal Information Processing Standards Publications 183 (FIPS). (December 1993). *Integration definition for function modelling, IDEF0.* Retrieved from http://www.idef.com/wp-content/uploads/2016/02/idef0.pdf.

Fedora and the Preservation of University Records Project. (2006). *Ingest guide for University electronic records.* Retrieved from https://dca.lib.tufts.edu/features/nhprc/reports/ingest/overview.html.

Feng, H., An, X., Liu, Y., & Dawson, A. (June 29–30, 2009). Challenges to e-government: Managing electronic records in China. In *The 9th European conference on e-government* (pp. 269–273). London: University of Westminster.

Finnell, J. (2011). *Records management theory's dilemma: What is record? Library Philosophy and Practice 2011 (December).* Retrieved from http://unllib.unl.edu/LPP/.

Fishery Glossary, FAO. (1996). Agro-ecological zoning: guidelines. *FAO Soils Bulletin,* 73.

Ford, A. (2009). *Modeling the environment* (2nd ed.). Washington DC: Island Press.

Foscarini, F. (2009). *Function-based records classification systems. An exploratory study of records management practices in central banks* (Ph.D. thesis). University Of British Columbia.

Franks, P. C. (2013). *Records and information management.* Chicago: American Library Association.

Fust, W., & Graf, C. (2002). *Foreword information and good governance.* Geneva: Swiss Federal Archives. Retrieved from http://www.deza.admin.ch/ressources/deza_product_e_418.pdf.

Gadomski, A. M. (2006). *An approach to a unified engineering meta-ontology. Universal domain paradigm: SPG representation of a domain-of-activity* The ENEA Agency MKEM Server (It). Retrieved from http://erg4146.casaccia.enea.it/wwwerg26701/gad-diag0.htm.

Garner, B. A. (2003). *Garner's Modern American Usage.* Oxford.
Greetham, G. (1999). Who's in, who's out: The cultural politics of archival exclusion. *Studies in the Literary Imagination, 32*(1), 1–28.
Goller, C., Löning, J., Will, T., & Wolff, W. (2000). Automatic document classification: A thorough evaluation of various methods. In *Internationales Symposiumfiir lnformation-swissenschafi(IS12000)* (pp. 145–162).
Guercio, M. (May 6–8, 2001). Records classification and content management: Old functions and new requirements in the legislations and standards for electronic record-keeping system. In *Proceedings of DLM-Forum 2002 access and preservation of electronic information: Best practices and solutions, Barcelona* (pp. 432–439). Retrieved from http://citeseerx.ist.psu.edu/viewdoc/downloaddoi=10.1.1.122.1484&rep=rep1&type=pdf#page=434.
Guercio, M. (2002). Principles, methods, and instruments for the creation, preservation, and use of archival records in the digital environment. *The American Archivist, 64*(2), 238–269.
Hardcastle, S. (1989). Providing storage facilities. In P. Emmerson (Ed.), *How to manage your records: A guide to effective practice.* Cambridge: ICSA Publishing.
Harmon, G. (1971). On the evolution of the information science. *Journal of the American Society for Information Science, 21,* 235–241.
HB 5031. (2011). *Australia records classification handbook.* Sydney: SAI Global Ltd.
Heaps, H. S. (1973). A theory of relevance for automatic document classification. *Information and Control, 22,* 268–278.
Heeks, R. (Ed.). (1999). *Reinventing government in the information age: International practice in IT-enabled public sector reform.* London: Routledge.
Heeks, R. (2003). Most e-government for development projects fail: How can risks be reduced? *IDPM i-Government Working 14th Series.* Retrieved from http://www.sed.manchester.ac.uk/idpm/research/publications/wp/igovernment/index.htm.
Henttonen, P., & Kettunen, K. (2011). Functional classification of records and organisational structure. *Records Management Journal, 21*(2), 86–103.
Hestenes, D. (1996). Modelling methodology for physics teachers. In *Proceedings of the international conference on undergraduate physics education* (pp. 1–22). College Park: Arizona State University. Retrieved from http://modeling.asu.edu/modeling/MODELING.PDF.
Hillston, J. (2003). *Model validation and verification. Teaching notes.* Retrieved from http://www.inf.ed.ac.uk/teaching/courses/ms/notes/note14.pdf.
Hjørland, B. (2008). Core classification theory: A reply to Szostak. *Journal of Documentation, 64*(3), 333–420.
Hjørland, B., & Pedersen, K. N. (2005). A substantive theory of classification for information retrieval. *Journal of Documentation, 61*(5), 582–597.
Hoshovsky, A. G., & Massey, R. J. (1968). Information science: Its ends, means, and opportunity. *Proceedings of the American Society for Information Science Annual Meeting, 5,* 47–55.
Hughes, M. (2000). *Mastering systems analysis and design.* Basingstoke: MacMillan.
Iacovino, L. (2004). Trustworthy shared electronic health records: Recordkeeping requirements and HealthConnect. *Journal of Law and Medicine, 12*(1), 40–59.
Idaho State University. (2006). *Records and information management.* Retrieved from http://www.isu.edu/infomgmt/program_scope.shtml.
IDEF. (1993). *Integration definition for function modeling (IDEF0).* Draft, federal information processing standards publication FIPSPUB 183. Springfield, Virginia: U.S. Department of Commerce.
International Council on Archives, ICA. (2008a). *Principles and functional requirements for records in electronic office environments. Module 2. Guidelines and functional requirements for electronic records management systems.* Paris: ICA. Retrieved from http://www.ica.org/en/node/38970.
International Council on Archives, ICA. (2008b). *Principles and functional requirements for records in electronic office environments. Module 3. Guidelines and functional requirements for in business systems.* Paris: ICA. Retrieved from http://www.ica.org/en/node/38968.

International Council on Archives, ICA. (2008c). *Principles and functional requirements for records in electronic office environments. Module 1. Overview and statement of principles*. Paris: ICA. Retrieved from http://www.ica.org/en/node/38972.

International Standard Organization, ISO 15489. (2001). *Information and documentation – Records management. Part 1: General; Part 2: Guidelines* (1st ed.).

International Standard Organization, ISO 16175-2. (2011). *Information and documentation – Principles and functional requirements for records in electronic office environments - Part 2: Guidelines and functional requirements for digital records management systems*.

InterPARES1. (2002). *Requirements for accessing and maintaining the authenticity for electronic records*. Retrieved from *http://www.interpares.org/book/interpares book k app02.pdf*.

InterPARES2. (2008). *InterPARES 2 terminology database*. Retrieved from *http://www.interpares.org/ip2/ip2 terminology db.cfm*.

Ismail, M. B. (2010). *Model kualiti perkongsian pengetahuan dalam organisasi awam dan kesannya ke atas pekerja serta penyampaian perkhidmatan*. Universiti Kebangsaan Malaysia (Ph.D. thesis).

Ismail, A., & Jamaludin, A. (2009). Towards establishing a framework for managing trusted records in the electronic environment. *Records Management Journal, 19*(2), 135–146.

Jenkinson, H. (1937). *A Manual of Archive Administration*. London: P. Lund, Humhries & co., ltd.

Jenkinson, H. (1965). *A manual of archive administration* (A reissue of the rev. 2nd ed. With introduction and bibliography by Roger H. Ellis). London: Percy Lund, Humphries & Co.

Jisc Infonet. (2012). *What is a record?* Retrieved from http://www.jiscinfonet.ac.uk/infokits/records-management/creation/what-is-a-record.

Johare, R., & Hussin, N. (2010). Conference proceeding: An analysis of best practice guidelines for developing recordkeeping functional requirements for the superior courts of Malaysia. In *InterPARES 3 international summit and symposium and ICA round table conference (CITRA), Oslo, Norway, September 17*.

Johnston, P. (1998). *Document structure, in effective records management project*. University of Glasgow. Retrieved from http://www.gla.ac.uk/infostrat/ERM/Docs/docstr.htm#Heading4.

Jones, K. S. (1970). Some thoughts on classification for retrieval. *Journal of Documentation, 26*(2), 89–101.

Jones, K. S. (2005). Revisiting classification for retrieval. *Journal of Documentation, 61*(5), 598–601.

Khan, R. (2006). *Introduction to library science*. New Delhi: SBS Publishers & Distributors Pvt. Ltd.

Krahn, K. (2012). *Looking under the hood: Unraveling the content, structure, and context of functional requirements for electronic recordkeeping systems* (Master thesis). University of Manitoba.

Kuhn, T. S. (1962). *The Structure of Scientific Revolutions*. Chicago: University of Chicago Press.

Lappin, J. (2011). *How MoReq2010 differs from previous electronic records management (ERM) system specifications*. Retrieved from http://thinkingrecords.co.uk/2011/05/06/how-moreq-2010-differs-from-previous-electronic-records-management-erm-system-specifications/.

Lewinson, P. (1939). Problems of archives classification. *The American Archivist, 23*(3), 297–310.

Library and Archives Canada (LAC). (2006a). *Function-based classification*. Retrieved from http://www.collectionscanada.gc.ca/government/products-services/007002-2084-e.html.

Library and Archives Canada. (2006b). *BASCS guidance*. Retrieved from http://www.collectionscanada.ca/information-management/002/007002-2091-e.html#one.

Lipchak, A. (2002). *Information management in support evidence-based government in the electronic age: Public policy forum discussion paper*. Retrieved from www.ppforum.ca/ow/ow_p_11_2002B_es.pdf.

Lipchak, A., & McDonald, J. (2003). *Electronic government and electronic records: E-records readiness and capacity building: An electronic discussion*. Retrieved from http://www.irmt.org/download/DOCUME~1/GLOBAL/discussionpaper.pdf.

Livelton, T. (1996). *Archival theory, records and the public.* Lanham: The Society of America Archivists and the Scarecrow Press, Inc.

Lowry, J., & Thurston, A. (2012). *Aligning records management with ICT/e-government and Freedom of Information in East Africa* Research Report at International Records Management trust. Retrieved from http://irmt.org/development-research/researchreports.

Lueders, D. (2013). *On why I no longer support the DoD 5015.2 standard.* Retrieved from http://www.aiim.org/community/blogs/expert/On-Why-I-No-Longer-Support-the-DoD-50152-Standard.

Lysakowski, R. (1997). The collaborative electronic notebook systems association (CENSA). In *Engineering in medicine and biology society. Proceedings of the 19th annual international conference of the IEEE, Chicago* (Vol. 6) (pp. 2659–2661).

MacLean, I. (1956). Trends in organising modern public records, with special reference to classification methods. *Archives & Manuscripts, 3*, 1–17.

MacNeil, H. (1994). Archival theory and practice: Between two paradigms. *Archivaria, 37*, 6–20.

MacNeil, H. (Fall 2002). Providing grounds for trust II: The findings of the authenticity task force of InterPARES. *Archivaria, 54*, 24–58.

Mai, J.-E. (2004). *Classifications on the web.* Retrieved from http://projects.ischool.washington.edu/chii/Publications/2004_ClassificationOfTheWeb.pdf.

Malaysian Administrative Modernisation and Management Planning Unit (MAMPU). (2003). *Standards, policies and guidelines-Malaysian government interoperability framework (MyGIF) Version 1.0.* Retrieved from http://www.mampu.gov.my/mampu/bm/program/ICT/ISPlan/ispdoc/Interoperability%20Framework.pdf.

Maltby, A. (1975). *Sayers' manual of classification for librarians* (5th ed.). London: Andre.

Marcia, L. Z. (2006). Sharing and use of subject authority data. *International Cataloging & Bibliographic Control, 35*(3), 52–54.

Martin, R. L. (1987). *Archival indexing: Problems and issues* (Master thesis). University of British Columbia.

McKemmish, S., Piggott, M., Reed, B., & Upward, F. (Eds.). (2005). *Archives: record keeping in society.* Wagga Wagga, Australia: Charles Sturt University, Centre for Information Studies.

McDonald, J. (1995). *Managing information in an office systems environment: The IMOSA project (58).* Spring, 142–153.

Millar, L. A. (2010). *Archives principles and practices.* London: Facet Publishing.

Milne, C. (2009). Developing information architectures through records management classification techniques. In *ISKO UK 2009 Conference, 22 –23 June.* Retrieved from http://www.iskouk.org/sites/default/files/milne_ISKOUK2009.pdf.

Mishra, P. N. (2010). *Principles of library and information science.* New Delhi: Alfa Publications.

Mitchell, T. W. (Ed.). (2003). *Norton on archives: the writings of Margaret Cross Norton on archival & records management.* Reissue. Chicago: Society of American Archivists.

Mnjama, N. (2004). Records and information: The neglected resource. *ESARBICA Journal: Journal of the Eastern and Southern Africa Regional Branch of the International Council on Archives, 23*, 44–59.

Mnjama, N., & Wamukoya, J. (2007). E-government and records management: An assessment tool for e-records readiness in government. *Records Management Journal, 5*(3), 274–284.

Moberg, Z. (1974). Automatic classification: directions of recent research. *Drexel library quarterly, 18*, 90–104.

Mokhtar, U. A., & Yusof, Z. M. (2009). Electronic records management in the Malaysian public sector: The existence of policy. *Records Management Journal, 9*(3), 231–244.

Morelli, J. (February 2005). *Business classification schemes: Issues and options.* (Vol. 124). Bulletin: Records Management Society.

MoReq. (2001). *Model requirements for the management of electronic records.* Retrieved from http://ec.europa.eu/archival-policy/moreq/doc/moreq_en.pdf.

MoReq2. (2008). *Model requirements for the management of electronic records: Update and extension.* Retrieved from http://ec.europa.eu/transparency/archival_policy.

MoReq2010. (2011). Modular requirements for records systems *Core services & plug-in modules* (Vol. 1). Retrieved from http://moreq2010.eu/pdf/moreq2010_vol1_v1_1_en.pdf.

Mokhtar, U. A., & Yusof, Z. M. (2015). Classification: The understudied concept. *International Journal of Information Management, 35*(2), 176–182.

Muller, G. (2007). *A multidisciplinary research approach.* Retrieved from http://www.gaudisite.nl.

Murdoch, W. (2007). To see archives plain: Reflections on recordkeeping and archives. *History of Intellectual Culture,* 7(1), 1–8.

National Archives and Records Administration (NARA). (2003). *Electronic records archives program management office, electronic records archives requirements document (RD), Version 2.0.* Retrieved from http://e-records.chrisprom.com/resources/standardsbestpractice/#sthash.MlAqijEB.dpuf.

National Archives of Australia. (2003). *Records management.* Retrieved from http://www.naa.gov.au/records-management/.

National Archives of Australia. (2008). *Specifications for electronic records management systems software and guidelines for implementing the specifications for electronic records management systems software (ERMS).* Retrieved from http://www.naa.gov.au/records-management/publications/ERMS-specs.aspx.

National Achieves of Australia (DIRKS). (2006a). *DIRKS manual.* Retrieved from http://www.naa.gov.au/recordkeeping/dirks/dirksman/contents.html.

National Achieves of Australia (DIRKS). (2006b). *The DIRKS manual: A strategic approach to managing business information.* Retrieved from http://www.naa.gov.au/recordkeeping/dirks/dirksman/dirks.html.

National Achieves of Australia (DIRKS). (2006c). *DIRKS: Step B – Analysis of business activity.* Retrieved from *http://www.naa.gov.au/recordkeeping/dirks/dirksman/step B.html.*

National Achieves of Australia (DIRKS). (2006d). *Functional specifications for electronic records management systems software.* Retrieved from http://www.naa.gov.au/recordkeeping/er/erms/specifications.html.

National Archives of Malaysia. (2008). *Electronic records management system: System specifications for public offices.* Retrieved from http://www2.arkib.gov.my/borang/Latest%20ERMS%20Specifications%20v1.9.pdf.

National Archives of Norway, NOARK 4. (2000). *Part 1 – Norwegian Recordkeeping System: Functional Description and Specification of Requirements.* Retrieved from http://arkivverket.no/eng/Public-Sector/Noark/Noark-4.

National Archives of Norway, NOARK 5. (2009). *Standard for Records Management.* Retrieved from http://arkivverket.no/eng/content/view/full/339.

National Information Technology Agenda (NITA). (1996). *National policy.* Retrieved from http://nitc.mosti.gov.my/nitc_beta/index.php/national-ict-policies/national-it-agenda-nita.

National Institute of Standards and Technology. (1993). *Federal Information Processing Standards 183 Publications for Integration Definition for Function Modelling (IDEF0).* Retrieved from http://www.idef.com/idef0.htm.

Nawi, H. S. A., Rahman, A. A., & Ibrahim, O. I. (2005). Government ICT project failure factors: Project stakeholders' views. *Journal of Information Systems Research and Innovation,* 69–77. Retrieved from http://seminar.utmspace.edu.my/jisri/.

Ngoepe, M. S. (2008). *An exploration of records management trends in the South African public sectors: A case study of the department of provincial and local* (Masters of Information Science thesis). University of South Africa.

Ngulube, P. (2004). Fostering accountability and justice: Opportunities for records managers in changing societies. *ESARBICA Journal: Journal of the Eastern and Southern Africa Regional Branch of the International Council on Archives, 23,* 23–32.

Ngulube, P. (2006). Nature and accessibility of public archives in custody of selected archival institutions in Africa. *ESARBICA Journal*, 25,106–124.

Nguyen, Swatman, Fraunholz, & Salzman (2009). EDRMS implementation in the Australian public sector. In *ACIS 2009: Evolving Boundaries and New Frontiers: Defining the IS Discipline: Proceedings of the 20th Australasian conference on Information Systems* (pp. 915–928). Retrieved from http://dro.deakin.edu.au/view/DU:30024943.

Norway Archives. (2002). *Public sector*. Retrieved from https://www.arkivverket.no/eng/Public-Sector.

Öberg, L.-M., & Borglund, E. (2006). What are the characteristics of records? *International Journal of Public Information Systems*, *2*(1), 55–76.

O'Brien, J. A. (2003). *Introduction to Information Systems: Essentials for the E-Business Enterprise*. Boston, MA: McGraw-Hill.

Orr, S.A. (2005). *Functions-based classification of records: Is it functional?* (Master thesis). University of Northumbria.

Palvia, S. C. J., & Sharma, S. S. (2007). *E-government and e-governance: Definitions/domains framework and status around the world*. Retrieved from www.iceg.net/2007/books.1/1-369.pdf.

Painter, A. F. (1974). Classification: Theory and practice. *Drexel Library Quarterly*, *10*(4), 125.

Parapadakis, G. (2013). *A clouded view of records and auto-classification*. Retrieved from http://4most.wordpress.com/2013/06/26/clouded-view-of-records-and-classification/.

Pearce-Moses, R. (2005). *Glossary of archival and records terminology (archival fundamentals series II)*. Chicago: Society of American Archivists.

Pearce-Moses, R., & Davis, S. E. (2008). *New skills for a digital era colloquium by National Archives and Records Administrations Society of American Archivists 31st May–2nd June 2006*. Washington, DC: Arizona State Library.

Perumpalath, B. P. (2005). *Modelling business process: An integrated approach* (MBA (International) thesis). Porthsmouth Business School.

Piggot, S. (2002). Evidence based governance in the electronic age. In *Paper presented at the 32nd annual conference of the association of Caribbean University Research and Institutional Libraries, Jamaica, 22 May–1 June*.

Presley, A., Sarkis, J., & Liles, D. H. (2000). A soft-systems methodology approach for product and process innovation. *IEEE Transactions on Engineering Management*, *47*(3), 379–392.

Public Record Office, (TNA). (1999). *Functional requirements*. Retrieved from http://collections.europarchive.org/tna/20080108102455/. *http://www.nationalarchives.gov.uk/electron icrecords/function.htm*.

Ramli, R. M. (2012). Malaysian e-government: Issues and challenges in public administration. In *International proceedings of economics development & research. Phnom Penh, Cambodia, September 28–29. EBSCOHOST* (Vol. 48(9)) (pp. 19–23).

Reed, B. (2008). Service Oriented Architectures and Recordkeeping. *Records Management Journal*, *18*(1), 7–20.

Richmond, P. A. (Spring 1960). Some Aspects of Basic Research in Classification. *Library Resources & Technical Services*.

Roberts, J. W. (1990). Archival theory: Myth or banality? *The American Archivist*, *53*(1), 110–120.

Robinson, C. (1999). Functional analysis and keyword classification. In *Managing change – A blueprint for the future, the Edmonton chapter of the Association of Records Managers and Administrators (ARMA). 2–3 March 1999 Alberta, Canada: Seminar, Edmonton*. Retrieved fromhttp://web.archive.org/web/20020623213601/www.records.nsw.gov.au/publicsector/rk/edmonton/functional_analysis1.htm.

Rotenstreich, S. (2006). *The differences between electronic documents and paper documents* (Teaching Notes). Retrieved from http://www.seas.gwu.edu/~shmuel/WORK/Differences/Chapter%203%20-%20Sources.pdf.

Rouse, M. (2005). *Definition of framework*. Retrieved from http://whatis.techtarget.com/definition/framework.

RSD. (n.d.). *The evolution from records management to information governance.* Retrieved from http://www.rsd.com/en/resources/infographics/evolution-information-governance.
Sabourin, P. (Spring 2001). Constructing a function-based records classification system: Business activity structure classification system. *Archivaria, 51,* 138–154.
Santangelo, J. (November/December 2009). Rise of the machines: The role of text analytics in records classification and disposition. *Information Management.* Retrieved from www.arma.org.
Saracevic, T. (1999). Information science. *Journal of the American Society for Information Science, 50*(12), 1051–1063.
Savic, D. (1995). Automatic classification of office documents: Review of available methods and techniques. *Records Management Quarterly – ARMA,* 3–18.
Schellenberg, T. R. (1956). *Modern archives principles and techniques.* Chicago: The University of Chicago Press.
Schellenberg, T. R. (1961). *Archival principles of arrangement.* Chicago: Society of American Archivists.
Schwartz, J. M., & Cook, T. (2002). Archives, records, and power: The making of modern memory. *Archival Science, 2*(1–2), 1–19.
Sedona Principles. (2003). *Best practices recommendations & principles for addressing electronic document production.* Sedona Conference. Retrieved from http://www.thesedonaconference.org/miscFiles/SedonaPrinciples200303.
Service Circular 5. (2007). *Office management guidelines, Chapter vi, vii and viii.* Retrieved from http://www2.arkib.gov.my/ksprj/index.phpoption=com_content&view=article&id=47&Itemid=68&lang=bm.
Shafie, S. (2007). A-government initiatives in Malaysia and the role of the national archives in digital records management. In *The 8th general conference of EASTICA & seminar, Tokyo, 21–26 October.* Retrieved from http://www.archives.go.jp/english/news/071115.html.
Shafie, S. (2014). *Penyediaan pra-syarat DDMS: Pembangunan klasifikasi fail fungsian.* Retrieved from www.arkib.gov.my/documents/10157/93f1a98e-f515-430d-8d4f-07c4d1d2ef85.
Shepherd, E., & Yeo, G. (2003). *Managing records: A handbook of principles and practice.* London: Facet Publishing.
Shipman, F. M., & McCall, R. (1994). *Supporting knowledge-base evolution with incremental formalization, Paper presented at the CHI 94.* Boston: Massachusetts, 285–291.
Shipman, F. M., & McCall, R. (1999). Incremental formalization with the hyper object substrate. *ACM Transactions on Information Systems, 17*(2), 199–227.
Shupak, H. (1974). Classification: A definition. *Drexel Library Quarterly, 10*(4), 4–10.
e-SPARK. (2008). *Guidelines for storing and preserving records in the public sectors.* Retrieved from http://www2.arkib.gov.my/english/elektronik.html.
Stapleton, R. (1983–84). Jenkinson and Schellenberg: A comparison. *Archivaria, 17,* 75–85 (Winter 1983–84).
Stevenson, G. (1974). The historical context: Traditional classification since 1950. *Drexel Library Quarterly, 10*(4), 11–20.
Sutton, A. (1980). Selected Writings of Sir Hilary Jenkinson. *Great Britain: Redwood Burn Limited Trowbridge and Esher.*
Szostak, R. (2004). *Classifying science, phenomena, data, theory, method, practice.* Dordrecht: Springer.
Szostak, R. (2008). Classification, interdisciplinary, and the study of science. *Journal of Documentation, 64*(3), 319–332.
Szostak, R. (2014). The importance of knowledge organization. *Bulletin of the Association for Information Science and Technology, 40,* 37–42. http://dx.doi.org/10.1002/bult.2014.1720400414.
Taylor, L. (2007). *Knowledge, information and the business process: Revolutionary thinking or common sense?* Oxford: Chandos Publishing.

Taylor, R. N., Medvidovic, N., & Dashofy, E. M. (2010). *Software Architecture: Foundations, Theory and Practice*. New Jersey: John Wiley & Sons, Inc.

The Pittsburgh Project (University of Pittsburgh Electronic Records Project). (1997). *Functional Requirements for Evidence in Recordkeeping. Variables in the Satisfaction of Archival Requirements for Electronic Records Management*. Pittsburgh, PA: University of Pittsburgh, School of Information Sciences.

The UBC Project. (1997). *The preservation of the integrity of electronic records (UBC-MAS Project)*. Retrieved from http://www.interpares.org/UBCProject/intro.htm.

Thomassen, T. (2001). A first introduction to archival science. *Archival Science, 1*(4), 373–385.

Todd, M. (2003). *Business classification scheme design*. Kew: The National Archives.

Tschan, R. (2002). A comparison of jenkinson and on appraisal. *Society of American Archivists, 65*(2), 176–195.

Underwood, W. E. (1997). Research issues in records management theory, modelling and practise. *Archives & Museum Informatics*. Retrieved from http://www.archimuse.com/erecs97/S3-bu.HTM.

United Kingdom Public Record Office. (2002). *Requirements for electronic records management systems*, 1–4 (Functional Requirements. Revision – Final Version).

United Nations E-Government Survey. (2012). *E-government for the people*. Retrieved from Unpan1.un.org/intradoc/groups/public/documents/un/unpan048065.pdf.

US Department of Defense. DoD 5015.02-STD. (2007). *Electronic records management software applications design criteria standard*. Retrieved from http://www.dtic.mil/whs/directives/corres/pdf/501502std.pdf.

Upward, F. (1998). *In search of the continuum: Ian MacLean's 'Australian experience' essays on recordkeeping*, 110–130. Retrieved from http://www.sims.monash.edu.au/research/rcrg/publications/fuptrc.html.

Wallace, D. (2004). Recordkeeping for accountability. *ESARBICA Journal: Journal of the Eastern and Southern Africa Regional Branch of the International Council on Archives, 23*, 17–22.

Wallace, P. E. (1987). *Records management: Integrated information system* (2nd ed.). New York: John Wiley & Sons.

Wamukoya, J., & Mutula, S. M. (2005). E-records management and governance in East and Southern Africa. *Malaysian Journal of Library & Information Science, 10*(2), 67–83.

Warland, A., & Lappin, J. (2011). MoReq2010-A specification that matters for the management of electronic records. *IQ: The RIM Quarterly, 27*(4), 28–31.

Webber, S. (2003). Information science in 2003: A critique. *Journal of Information Science, 29*(4), 311–330.

World Bank Website. (2005). *Definition of e-government*. Retrieved from http://www1.worldbank.org/publicsector/egov/definition.htm.

Women's Centre for Change. (2014). *Divorce (Syariah Law)*. Retrieved from http://www.wccpenang.org/files/docs/syariah-divorce.pdf.

Xie, L. (2006). *Evaluation of the electronic document and record management program in a Canadian municipality* (Master thesis). University of British Columbia.

Xie, L. (2007). *Function-based records classification system: A comparative study*. Retrieved from http://www.armaedfoundation.org/pdfs/Sherry_Xie_Study.pdf.

Xie, L. (2008). Electronic records management: The missing player in the eGov movement. In *Proceedings of the 4th international conference on e-government, RMIT Univ. Melbourne, Australia, 23–24 Oct. 2008* (pp. 481–486). Reading: Academic Publishing Ltd.

Yaacob, R. A., & Sabai, R. M. (2011). Electronic records management in Malaysia: A case study in one government agency. In *Asia Pacific conference library & information education & practice. Putrajaya, Malaysia, June 21–22, 2011*. Retrieved from http://fim.uitm.edu.my/a-liep2011.

Yeo, G. (2007). Concepts of record (1): Evidence, information, and persistent representations. *The American Archivist, 70*, 315–343 (Fall/Winter 2007).
Yusof, Z. M. (2009). Nurturing attitudes for records management in Malaysia financial institution. *Records Management Journal, 19*(3), 218–230.
Yusof, Z. M., & Chell, R. W. (2000). The records life cycle: An inadequate concept for technology-generated records. *Information Development, 16*(3), 135–141.
Yusof, Z. M., & Chell, R. W. (2002). Towards a theoretical construct for records management. *Records Management Journal, 12*(2), 55–64.
Yusof, Z. M., & Chell, R. W. (2005). *Issues in records management*. Bangi: Penerbit UKM.
Zouridis, S., & Thaens, M. (2003). E-government: Towards a public administration approach. *The Asian Journal of Public Administration, 25*(2), 159–183.

FURTHER READING

Connaway, L. S., & Powell, R. R. (2010). *Basic research methods for librarians* (5th ed.). Littleton, CO: Libraries Unlimited.
Cooper, D. R., & Schindler, P. S. (2001). *Business research methods* (7th ed.). New York: McGraw-Hill.
Cooper, H. M. (1988). The structure of knowledge synthesis. *Knowledge in Society, 1*, 104–126.
Department of Syariah Judiciary Malaysia (DSJM). (2011). *Website portal*. Retrieved from http://www.esyariah.gov.my/portal/page/portal/Portal%20ESyariah%20BI/Portal%20E-Syariah%20Profil%20JKSM.
Garger, J. (2010). *Using the case study method in Ph.D. research*. Retrieved from http://www.brighthub.com/education/postgraduate/articles/77789.aspx.
George, A. L., & Bennett, A. (2005). *Case studies and theory development in the social sciences*. Cambridge, MA: MIT Press.
Hinkelmann, K. (2008). *Classification schemes. Hand-out notes*. University of Applied Sciences North-Western Switzerland. Fall Semester 2008/2009. Retrieved from http://www.hinkelmann.ch/knut/lectures/irko/.
Hirtle, P. B. (2000). *Archival in a digital age*. Council on Library and Information Resources. Retrieved from http://www.clir.org/pubs/reports/pub92/contents.html.
Kunde, N. (Spring/Summer 2009). Getting it done – Collaboration and development of the digital records conversion standard. *The American Archivist, 72*, 146–169.
Lauesen, S., & Vinter, O. (2001). Preventing requirement defects: An experiment in process improvement. *Requirements Engineering Journal, 6*(1), 37–50.
Leedy, P., & Ormrod, J. (2001). *Practical research: Planning and design* (7th ed.). Upper Saddle River, NJ: Merrill Prentice Hall.
Livelton, T. (1991). *Public records: A study in archival theory* (Master thesis). University of British Columbia.
Mahathir, M. (2003). *Majlis pelancaran e-Syariah*. Retrieved from http://www.pmo.gov.my/ucapan/?m=p&p=mahathir&id=304.
Mai, J.-E. (2000). *The subject indexing process: An investigation of problems in knowledge representation* (Ph.D. thesis) University of Texas. Retrieved from http://jenserikmai.info/Papers/2000_PhDdiss.pdf.
Mai, J.-E. (2002). Is classification theory possible? Rethinking classification research. *Advances in Knowledge Organization, 8*, 472–478. Retrieved from http://jenserikmai.info/Papers/2002_IsClassificationTheoryPossible.pdf.
Malaysia. (2003). *Rekod Elektronik dan Akta Arkib Negara 2003* (Arkib Negara Malaysia).
Manoff, M. (2004). Theories of the archive from across the disciplines. *Libraries and the Academy, 4*(1), 9–25.
McLeod, J., & Hare, C. (2006). *How to manage records in the e-environment* (2nd ed.). London: Routledge Taylor & Francis Group.

Mertens, D. M. (2010). *Transformative research and evaluation*. New York: Guilford.

Mitchell, T. W. (1975). *The writings of Margaret Cross Norton on archival and records management*. Carbondale: Southern Illinois University Press.

Muller, S., Feith, J. A., & Fruin, R. (1968). *Manual for arrangement and description of archives* (2nd ed.) (Arthur H. Leavitt, Trans.). New York: H.W. Wilson Co.

Neuman, W. L. (2010). *Social research methods: Qualitative and quantitative approaches* (7th ed.). Upper Saddle River: Pearson Education (US).

Pemberton, J. M. (1997). Canadian information professionals sound the ALARM and ARMA and SAA reach out. *Records Management Quarterly*, *31*(4), 68–73.

Presley, A., Sarkis, J., & Liles, D. (1997). A multi-criteria justification methodology. *Journal of Engineering Valuation and Cost Analysis*, *1*(2), 111–123.

Ridener, J. (2009). *From polders to postmodernism: A concise history of archival theory*. Minnesota: Litwin Books.

Robson, C. (2011). *Real world research* (3rd ed.). London: John Wiley & Sons.

Schutt, R. K. (2012). *Investigating the social world: The process and practise of research* (7th ed.). Boston: Sage Publications, Inc. University of Massachusetts.

Shields, P., & Tajalli, H. (2006). Intermediate theory: The missing link in successful student scholarship. *Journal of Public Affairs Education*, *12*(3), 313–334. Retrieved from http://ecommons.txstate.edu/polsfacp/39/.

Singh, P., Klobas, J. E., & Anderson, K. (2007). Information seeking behaviour of ERMS users. Implications for records management practices. *Human Information Technology*, *9*(1), 135–181.

INDEX

'*Note*: Page numbers followed by "f" indicate figures and "t" indicate tables.'

D

E

F

G

H

I

FSC
www.fsc.org
MIX
Papier | Fördert
gute Waldnutzung
FSC® C083411

Kolibri 360 GmbH
Ferdinand-Jühlke-Straße 7
99095 Erfurt, Deutschland
produktsicherheit@kolibri360.de